SOUTH CAROLINA IRISH

ARTHUR MITCHELL

THE History PRESS

Published by The History Press
Charleston, SC 29403
www.historypress.net

First published 2011

Manufactured in the United States

ISBN 978.1.60949.187.1

Library of Congress Cataloging-in-Publication Data

Mitchell, Arthur, 1936-
South Carolina Irish / Arthur Mitchell.
p. cm.
Includes bibliographical references.
ISBN 978-1-60949-187-1
1. Irish--South Carolina--History. 2. Irish Americans--South Carolina--History. I. Title.
F280.I6M58 2011
305.891'620757--dc22
2010053833

Contents

Preface

When I came to South Carolina in January 1976 to become a history professor at the Salkehatchie Campus of the University of South Carolina (USC), I already had a strong interest in the role of Irish people in this country. I assumed, however, that the impact of the Irish was very much a northern urban phenomenon, as in my native Boston, but I decided, making the best of things, to do some investigation into the history of the Irish and Scotch-Irish in the Palmetto State. Initially, I was only finding traces of such through library research, so I went to the archives of the South Carolina Historical Society in Charleston. Looking out a window of the Fireproof Building, I observed across Meeting Street a large Greek revival building with a sizeable harp on its pediment. Hotfooting it across the street, I met Carl Pulkinen, the president of the Hibernian Society of Charleston, who, on the spot, invited me to write a history of this organization, which traces its origins to providing assistance to refugees in the wake of the 1798 Rebellion in Ireland. After frequent and most enjoyable visits to the Holy City emerged a book that the society published in 1982.

With the encouragement and assistance of several people, including John J. Duffy of USC, David Heisser of the Citadel, Donald Williams of the Hibernian Society and others, I continued to assemble all kinds of material on the subject and wrote some articles on it, but no major composition resulted. Other historical areas drew my attention.

My consuming interest in Boston politics and my near fascination with John Fitzgerald Kennedy resulted in *JFK and His Irish Heritage*, which was produced by Moytura Press in Dublin in 1993. *Revolutionary Government in*

Ireland: Dail Eireann, 1919–1922, which appeared in 1995, grew out of my graduate studies at Trinity College, Dublin. Inspired by the knowledge that my great-grandfather Patrick Gallagher, an illiterate, unskilled immigrant, had served (briefly) in the Union army during the Civil War and was at (or near) Gettysburg got me going on the rise of the Irish to political power in Boston beginning in the 1880s, a subject that I intend to finish into a book (shortly). Though not much of a soldier myself, I continued to be drawn to the subject, particularly if it had an Irish aspect to it. Working with Dr. David Doyle of University College, Dublin, I assembled about thirty articles by the best historians I could find, the result of which (at last) will be *Irish Soldiers, American Wars: Irish Involvement from the Mexican War to the Indian Wars*, forthcoming in 2011. This military history preoccupation went further, with the production this spring of a long article, "Observations on the Korean War: American Triangle—Korea, Formosa and China." During the course of my research, I found that the Koreans were sometimes described as the "Irish of the Far East" for the resolute and fiery spirit of that people. (While in Greece recently, I was told that Greek people sometimes see themselves as the Irish of the Mediterranean, for similar reasons but with some emphasis on contentiousness.) Growing out of trips to Germany with my good friend, colleague and fellow historian Joseph Siren and my lifelong interest in Nazi Germany came *Hitler's Mountain: The Fhurer, Obersalzberg and the American Occupation of Berchtesgaden*, published by McFarland in Jefferson in the North Carolina mountains in 2007.

Which reminds me of my proclivity to find an Irish angle wherever possible. Giving a talk on Hitler in the Bavarian mountains, I was challenged—rather snidely I thought—to find such an aspect. I quickly informed this heckler that, with a bit of forbearance, I would be telling her about the marriage of Hitler's half brother Alois to Bridget Dowling, a quite stereotypical Irish woman, which in time produced Patrick Hitler, who, after making a pest of himself in Germany during the 1930s, immigrated to the United States (and whose family connections caused difficulties when he volunteered for military service during World War II—military recruiter: "Your uncle is *who*?"). But I digress.

Since I began digging up material on the Irish in this region of the country, having written entries on the Irish in both South and North Carolina for the *Encyclopedia of the Irish in America*, many articles have been written by a variety of historians, but the only major work that has been produced is by David Gleeson, in his excellent *The Irish in the South, 1815–1877* (2001).

In his otherwise authoritative *South Carolina: A History* (1998), based on understandably scanty sources, Walter Edgar declares that Irish people in this state had a rather unfortunate experience, which is not how I view it. Arguably, what *is* unfortunate is that not enough has been written about them (and possibly too much has been written about some of the other groups). That situation will now be remedied, forthwith!

Go *raibh mile maith agat* (thousands of thanks) to all who helped me with the work, in particular Denis Bergin, John J. Duffy, David Gleeson, David Heisser, Jim Lawracy, Carl Pulkinen, Donald Williams and Chris Woods; for so much library assistance, Sherrill Pinckney and Dan Johnson; and Jessica Berzon, commissioning editor, and Jaime Muehl, senior editor, at The History Press. Having been the recipient of research grants from the university and support from my campus, as well as being given the "Irish Carolinian" award by Irish organizations in Charleston in March 2010, it was time to finish the book I had been working on all along—a narrative about that lively, provocative and imaginative people, the ménage of people from Erin's Isle and their descendants who took root in the Carolinas. *Slante na Gael* (Health of the Gaels)!

Introduction

The Irish in South Carolina

When the matter of the Irish in America is raised, one almost automatically thinks of their presence in the port and industrial areas of the Northeast and Midwest, a phenomenon that largely dates to the famine era of the late 1840s. In the colonial period, however, there was a much greater concentration of Irish people in the South, particularly in South Carolina and Georgia and then in Tennessee and Kentucky.

In the Carolinas, Irish people of all sorts have left their mark on history and culture, from Murphy Island above Charleston to the town of Murphy at the western tip of North Carolina. The prominence of Irish people there is seen in a phrase still remembered in Charleston: "Said the governor of North Carolina to that of South Carolina, 'It's a long time between drinks.'" This statement refers to the role of two Galway-born kinsmen—Thomas Burke, who was governor of North Carolina during the Revolution, and Aedanus Burke, who, although not a governor of South Carolina, was a leader in the Patriot cause in the Palmetto State, serving as a military officer, congressman and high court judge. What is remarkable about the two Burkes is that, although recent arrivals, both rose to leadership in the upheaval of the Revolution in the Carolinas.[1]

The central reality of life in South Carolina was that, at least until 1930, it had a black majority. Among those from Europe, other than the English, there were only two groups in sizeable numbers, and probably there were as many German as Irish emigrants and their descendants. But given the Irish propensity for volatility and their love of politics as theater, those from Ireland, of whatever sort, had a much greater impact than the other groups.

Irish people had more importance in South Carolina than in adjoining North Carolina, so this work is about their role in the Palmetto State, with an appendix addressing their presence in North Carolina. In his recent comprehensive history of South Carolina, Walter Edgar, referring to the colonial period, declares, "There were a considerable number of Irish in South Carolina, and their tale is not a pleasant one" due to the various restrictions on their religious and political status at that time. A major reason for this assessment is that scholarly history (and little of the other kind) has not been produced about Irish immigration or the impact of other ethnic groups in the Palmetto State. Although they faced many difficulties, as almost all immigrants did, the Irish stream continued, and they became part of the fabric of the community that constitutes South Carolina.[2]

I

The First Irish Migration

From the very beginning of the colony in 1670, Irish people in South Carolina have constituted a small but significant part of the European population. Considerable attention has been given to the Huguenot and Scottish element in the state; now it is time to focus on the Irish.

Referring to the flow of Irish people into Carolina in the colonial period, David Ramsay declared in 1793, "Of all countries none has furnished the province with so many inhabitants as Ireland. Scarce a ship sailed from any of its ports for Charleston that was not crowded with men, women and children." He noted that "many causes may be assigned for this spirit of emigration from Ireland, but domestic oppression was the most powerful and prevalent." Incorporated in the movement of Irish people to America in the period leading up to the Revolution and beyond was a powerful strand of transatlantic republican radicalism from both Ireland and Britain that was manifested in strong Irish support for American independence and the subsequent revolutionary United Irishmen movement in Ireland, which spilled over to the United States in the early period of the American republic.[1]

Irish immigration to South Carolina was concentrated in the period from 1730 to 1775. It was the major site of settlement of Irish people in the southern colonies. A majority of those from Ireland were from the northern province of Ulster, the so-called Scotch-Irish, but there was also a sizeable number of immigrants of the older Irish stock from all parts of that country. That more of the Catholic Irish group did not come in this period was due, in part, to the general hostility to Roman Catholicism in the colonies. In the early years of the eighteenth century, the South Carolina Assembly attempted to block immigration of Catholic Irish, but the legislation was disallowed by the colony's proprietors, who viewed it as an encroachment on their rights.[2]

After a royal charter for the Carolina colony was issued in 1663, the new proprietors began a search for potential settlers. Although they certainly were not the first choice, the search apparently extended to Irish people of the original stock, stubbornly Catholic in religion. However, the agent for the proposed colony in 1667 found that these people were "loth [*sic*] to leave the smoke of their cabins."[3]

Captain Florence O'Sullivan, from Kinsale, County Cork, for whom Sullivan's Island is named, was one of the original settlers in the Carolina colony in 1670. He previously had been involved in voyages to Barbados and collected a group of twelve indentured servants at Kinsale who took part in the 1670 settlement convoy. Among these were James Donaghue, Hannah Forgetee, Matthew Dowling and Brian Fitzpatrick.[4]

Local legend has it that when O'Sullivan first came ashore, he was greeted by a native Irishman—a "Mr. O'Possum." Landowner, legislator, Indian fighter and first surveyor general, O'Sullivan was an energetic and controversial figure. One of his contemporaries, the famous John Locke, characterized him as "dissentious, troublesome; bound to the peace and good behavior; exactor of unreasonable fees; no able surveyor; knavish…disliked; unfit; ignorant in surveying; of no understanding…Ill natured buggerer of children…A very ill man." Another of O'Sullivan's critics charged that he "doth by his absurd language abuse the Governor, Council and Country and by his rash and base dealings…hath caused everyone in the country almost to be his enemy." Yet another noted "the trouble Captain Sullivan hath put this colony into by his ignorance, whose ill fate is to profess much and to perform nothing."

The litany of O'Sullivan's alleged failings, probably due to his close connection to some of the proprietors, did not prevent him from continuing his active involvement in the life of the colony. As a member of the provincial parliament, he was appointed to man a signal cannon at the mouth of the harbor. When a Spanish fleet came into his sight, he fired the gun and sent up five columns of smoke to indicate how many ships were approaching. As the first surveyor general, in 1680 he was granted 2,340 acres of land on the island that bears his name, as well as in the area that later became Mount Pleasant. In 1684, he joined with his successor as surveyor general in stimulating a disturbance in Charleston. According to Yates Snowden:

> *It is reported that O'Sullivan, who had been placed in charge of the cannon on the island that bears his name, in order to alarm the town in case of the appearance off the bar of any Spanish ships, being desperately short of provisions, deserted his charge and joined with Culpepper in the Charles Town disturbance. As he was considered the more culpable of the two, he was arrested by the town marshal for sedition and required to give security for his good conduct.*

Yet he retained office in the colonial government. He remained an officer in the militia through 1676 and was commissioner of public accounts in 1682–83. He willed his land to his daughter Katherine.

The Charleston novelist William Gilmore Simms sees O'Sullivan as an important figure in the origins of Carolina. He contends that O'Sullivan's work on building the defensive facility at the entrance to Charleston Harbor marked him as a man of vision. According to Simms, himself the son of an exiled Irishman, O'Sullivan "spoke with a decided Irish accent" and was a "Celt of characteristic courage." His part in a minor revolt against colonial authority had a much greater significance. Simms viewed this episode as a "tendency to see Celts as the catalysts of change from a hereditary aristocratic South ruled by and for Anglo-Normans, at the expense of politically and culturally subdued Celts, to a more 'democratic' South in which any free man might succeed and make of himself a gentleman." Patrick Melvin, who has done the most to investigate the activities of O'Sullivan, grants him the following accolade: "His seafaring and soldiering background in the West Indies gave him the necessary qualities for a venture which could be threatened by natural and human obstacles." The subsequent career of the redoubtable captain is lost to history.[5]

O'Sullivan obviously was not Scotch-Irish. Neither was this true of John Barnwell, a native of Dublin for whom Barnwell County is named, who was part of the Protestant Anglo-Irish group that began to arrive in the early eighteenth century.[6]

In the list of land warrants from the establishment of the colony until 1711, there are about thirty names that are of old-stock Irish origins (not Scotch-Irish). These include Michael Bourke (or Burke), Philip Brady, George Cantey, Teague Cantey, John Cantey, John Carr, John Carroll, Peter Collins, John Conway, Bryan Fitzpatrick, Edward Flaharty, Robert Flood, James Fogarty, Edward Hearn, Thomas Holland, Brian Kelly, Richard Kennedy, Thomas Lynch, Thomas McLaughlin, Michael Mahon, James

Moore, Florence O'Sullivan (of course) and Thomas Lane. This indicates a greater Irish presence at that time than is usually recognized.[7]

Bryan or Brian Fitzpatrick, one of the servants assembled by O'Sullivan, became a landowner. Termed "a noted villain," he was involved with the killing of an Indian in 1671 or 1672. Efforts to arrest him failed, and he fled to St. Augustine, where he informed Spanish authorities that he had been persecuted as a Roman Catholic and revealed that the Carolina colony contained eight hundred white people and three hundred Negroes. This information was used by the Spanish in a subsequent attack on the settlement.[8]

Teague Cantey arrived from parts unknown in Ireland, via Barbados, in 1672, two years after his son George. He received warrants for a considerable amount of land but died in 1679. According to a later writer, Joseph S. Ames, the inventory of Teague Cantey's estate, with its bill of expenses for wine and rum in connection with a funeral, would seem to plainly indicate that the family was of Irish descent. The Canteys played a continuing role in the development of South Carolina.[9]

As was the case in the "mother" colony of Barbados, the Carolina colony succeeded too well in its original purpose—to exploit land through the use of African slave labor. A black majority quickly emerged. Anthony Ashley Cooper, one of the original proprietors, saw the need to stimulate the immigration of white people. He was responsible for generating a series of promotional pamphlets, widely distributed in England and Ireland, declaring that there was excellent opportunity to cultivate olives, wines, figs and silk in Carolina, which would preclude England's dependence on imports from the Mediterranean.

The basic problem with the efforts of Cooper and other Carolina promoters was that they were seeking politically reliable Englishmen, and few of these were forthcoming. Their attention turned to England's other island, with its growing population. In the north of Ireland, there was a mass of newly planted Presbyterians of Scottish origin, and many of them did take the bait. But these people were certainly not English, and their religious orientation bred a spirit of opposition to almost everything English. In time, they became known in American history as the Scotch-Irish. Along with them came people from other parts of Ireland.[10]

The great majority in Ireland was a mass of impoverished, landless people of Roman Catholic religion, few of whom could be enticed to sail across a dangerous ocean to a wild frontier settlement. Oliver Cromwell's forced migration of thousands of Irish people to the Caribbean in the 1640s was a vivid memory. Moreover, it was not advisable to leave rural areas for port cities due to the danger of being forcibly transported to "Amerikay."[11]

Some people from other colonies were drawn to Carolina. In 1696, Peter O'Kelley, his wife and their six children joined a group from Dorchester, Massachusetts, that migrated to the area since named Dorchester County, South Carolina. A Patrick O'Kelley from this district was a soldier in the Revolution.[12]

In the 1730s, the colonial government established a township plan, funded by a tax on imported slaves, to encourage immigration and expansion. In 1737, however, the arrival of a large number of Irish people quickly exhausted the fund. Despite an ensuing political controversy concerning the tax issue, apparently the immigrants were left to fend for themselves. It was at this time that large numbers of Irish people settled in the Newberry, Camden and Williamsburg areas.[13]

A renewed effort to secure Irish servants was undertaken by the proprietors in the 1680s. Two pamphlets extolling the virtues of the colony were printed in Dublin at that time. One of these—a fifty-page booklet produced in 1684—listed departures from seven Irish ports that year. In the best tradition of real estate advertising, it extolled the natural riches of the land, declared that Carolina was "not near so hot as in Virginia" and said that there was "a perfect friendship with the Indians." It drew to the attention of prospective immigrants the fact that the proprietors were providing generous land grants.[14]

"Thinking that a governor from abroad would be more devoted to their interests," the proprietors appointed Irishman Richard Kyrle as governor in 1684. A timber merchant and knight in Cork, it was said that Kyrle "knew nothing of the people or their wants" in the colony, but during his short administration "there was a considerable emigration movement from Ireland." He died the following year, apparently another victim of southern heat and disease.[15]

Alarmed by the rising African slave population, the Carolina Assembly, in 1698, authorized the payment of bounties to anyone who could bring Europeans, indentured or not, into the colony. There was only one qualification in this offer: "Irish only excepted." The position of "No Irish need apply" has long antecedents.[16]

Another Irish-born governor was James Moore, a descendant of Roger Moore, a leader in the 1641 rebellion in Ireland. He arrived in Charleston around 1675. "The blood of his rebellious ancestors seemed to evidence itself in Moore's own activities, for he soon identified himself with the discontented elements and was active in movements of protest…A needy, forward and ambitious man," he took advantage of the death of the incumbent governor to get the colonial assembly to elect him as the successor in 1700 and served until 1703. After further warfare with the Indians, he died in 1706.[17]

His son, General James Moore, known as "the outlaw of Goose Creek," led the revolutionary effort that ended the proprietors' control of the colony in 1719, whereupon he became governor with "the loudest acclamations of the populace" and served until 1721. He was the Speaker of the colonial assembly when he died in 1724.[18]

Three Irishmen—John Gough, Dominick Arthur and Michael Mahon—arrived from Barbados and in 1707 purchased the Cypress Barony of thirteen thousand acres in Berkeley County from Landgrave Peter Colleton. A native of Limerick in Ireland, Mahon called his thirty-five hundred acres Limerick Plantation. An adjoining area was called Irishtown "for a number of years before the end of 18th century." Irishtown was the setting, in 1748, for an alleged plot by some slaves to mount a rebellion. After a lengthy investigation, Thomas Aiken, the owner of the Irishtown plantation, concluded that the origins of the plot story began with four gossipy slave women.[19]

After a series of upheavals, the Harleston/Coming family became substantial plantation owners in Carolina. Some of the Harleston family had fled from England to Ireland in the 1640s to escape the wrath of Oliver Cromwell and his army. They already owned 700 acres near Dublin. After Affra Harleston married John Coming in 1671, they sailed to the colony to assemble land for farming. Since the colonial constitution granted 150 acres to anyone who brought a worker of some sort, and Coming brought with him six indentured servants, at least some of whom were Irish, he secured 900 acres. Trouble soon erupted with three of the bonded workers, centering on Philip O'Neil, who was accused of "threatening to overset the Boate wherein [Affra] was, and by taking food from her hands and throwing it to some dogs." Going further, O'Neil threatened to run away and join the Indians. For this gross misbehavior, he was sentenced to be tied to a tree for "one and twenty lashes upon his naked back." Proprieties were to be observed.[20]

John Barnwell arrived in 1701. He was probably the son of alderman Matthew Barnwell of Dublin, a captain in the army of James II who was killed in the Siege of Derry in 1690. In Charleston, young Barnwell quickly rose to hold important administrative positions and, rising to the rank of colonel, was an effective fighter against the Indians and Spaniards. The general lack of an Irish presence can be observed in John Lawson's 1709 study of Carolina wildlife, in which he noted a species of fish—a perch. "They are called Irishmen, being freckled or mottled with black and blue spots."[21]

In 1716, five hundred Irish Protestants, encouraged by a generous land offer of the colonial assembly, settled the Yemassee lands. Three years later, the proprietors claimed the area for themselves with the result that "the unfortunate Irish emigrants, having spent the little money they had, many of them, reduced to poverty, perished, and the remainder moved to the northern colonies."[22]

The pressing need to increase the population was addressed by Governor Robert Johnson when he put forward, in 1730, a land settlement plan for several European groups. A settlement for Irish Protestants at Williamsburg (named for William of Orange), near the Santee River, was begun with an area of twenty square miles. In his history of South Carolina and Georgia published in 1779, Alexander Hewatt comments on this community:

> *Multitudes of labourers and husbandmen in Ireland, oppressed by landlords and bishops, and unable by their utmost diligence to procure a comfortable sustenance for their families, embarked for Carolina…But notwithstanding the bounty of the crown, these poor emigrants remained for several years in low and miserable circumstances.*

A Dublin newspaper announced in 1733 the impending departure of the *Charming Sally*, which would arrive "within twenty miles of the Irish settlement."[23]

In 1751, a small group of Irish Quakers, from Timahoe, County Kildare, established a community at Mulberry on the Wateree River. This is the Milhous connection of Richard M. Nixon. A Friends monthly meeting was maintained until the early 1780s, by which time the Irish Quakers had dispersed, with some of their members moving to North Carolina and Virginia.[24]

The colony launched several bounty schemes directed at the Protestant Irish in the 1760s. These included money payments for each immigrant and land grants to heads of families. The bounty of 1767 included free passage. These attractions undoubtedly were largely responsible for the increased emigration from Ireland in the period leading up to the Revolution. In procuring indentured servants to cross the broad Atlantic from Belfast to Charleston in mid-winter of 1766, William Beatty advertised the advantages of such a voyage, informing would-be emigrants that he would

> *clothe them in a genteel manner, pay their passage, and take care to have them happily settled in that country, where industry is amply rewarded and*

> *poverty is a stranger: therefore all young girls and spirited lads that choose to accompany him under these circumstances are desired to apply to him without loss of time, that their clothing and other things may be properly provided to their liking.*

A virtual holiday cruise—hurry, hurry, limited time offer! It appears that some of the emigrants who paid their own way on the vessel were those who shortly applied for a bounty of five pounds per head and land grants.[25]

After 1760, Irish immigration shifted from the Lowcountry to the western hill area as the Scotch-Irish moved down the Appalachians. According to D.D. Wallace, this group "fairly swarmed into the up country." The townships of Belfast, Londonderry and Boonesborough were designated for Irish Protestants, and thousands of Irish settlers moved down to the backcountry from Pennsylvania through the Great Valley of Virginia. Speaking of this period, Wallace comments, "This was mainly the Scotch-Irish, as the 1730s and '40s were mainly the German era."[26]

At this time, Irish-born Anglican clergyman Charles Woodmason began his work as a missionary in the backcountry. He denounced the action of the colonial legislature in spending £30,000 "to bring over 5 or 6000 Ignorant, mean, worthless, beggerly Irish Presbyterians, the Scum of the Earth, and Refuse of Mankind, and this solely to balance the Emigration of People from Virginia, who are all of the Established Church." He reported that he had been subjected repeatedly to "Insolences and Audacity," not only by Irish Presbyterians but also by New Light Baptists.

His troubles were legion. Children were allowed run "wild here like Indians—but as their Parents are Irish Presbyterians, they rather chuse [*sic*] to let them thus run wild, than to have them instructed in the Principles of Religion by a Minister of the Church of England." And it was not just the children:

> *The Young Women have a most uncommon Practice, which I cannot break them of. They draw their Shift as tight as possible to the Body, and pin it close to shew* [sic] *the roundness of their Breasts, and slender Waists (for they are generally finely shaped) and draw their Petticoat close to their hips to shew the fineness of their Limbs—so that they might as well be in* Puri Naturalibus—*Indeed Nakedness is not censurable or indecent here.*

One of his efforts at religious instruction caused him considerable distress. Although "a vast Body of People Assembled…After Service they went to Reveling, Drinking, Singing, Dancing and Whoring—and most of the Company were drunk before I quited [*sic*] the Spot." On another occasion, he had a very different experience: "From Lynch's Creek I crossed the Country by Way of Beaver Creek and gave a Sermon there to the New Imported Irish, who behav'd very reverently, and were very thankful." Woodmason's experiences are often quoted in studies of that kind. There must have been others![27]

In the mid-nineteenth century, advocates of the designation "Scotch-Irish" made a case that this group of people was separate and distinct from the emigrants from other parts of Ireland, who were overwhelmingly Catholic and nationalist in politics. The Scotch-Irish proponents described their people as sturdy, sober, hardworking farmers, Presbyterian in religion. Historian David Doyle has pointed out that this was not the frequent perception of this group by their contemporaries. He also points to the fact that in the 1800 census of five million people in the United States, only fifteen thousand listed themselves as Presbyterian. It seems to be the case that, with the dearth of church organization and clergy, frontiersmen adopted their own religious units or none at all.

Another historian, Leroy Eid, has rolled out evidence that this sizeable element was generally as Woodmason had found it. Eschewing tillage, these people preferred the pastoral practice of the casual grazing of animals. They developed a reputation for violence, whiskey distilling and casual living. In his account of Ireland in the 1770s, Arthur Young declared that the Ulster dissenters "were principally idle people, who far from being missed, left the country the better by their absence." This would appear to be a description of Andrew Jackson's community of a cluster of mean log cabins at Waxhaw. Eid concludes that the early flow of people from Ulster, as well as from other parts of Ireland, reflected the lifestyle and living conditions of the people there, and these were perpetuated when they ventured into the welcoming hills of the Appalachians. In their "Celtic theory" of southern distinctiveness, Forrest McDonald and Grady McWhiney have argued that this mass of Irish, Scotch-Irish and any other kind of Irish forged the identity and mentality of the region. Not a historian but an acute observer of the South, Wilbur Cash termed the region the "Celtic South."[28]

So what happened to all the Ulster Presbyterians claimed by various historians? This raises questions about the denominational attachment, or lack thereof, of these people before they left Ulster. There is no evidence that Andrew Jackson's family from outside of Carrickfergus had any connection with organized religion. Certainly, independent religious organizations

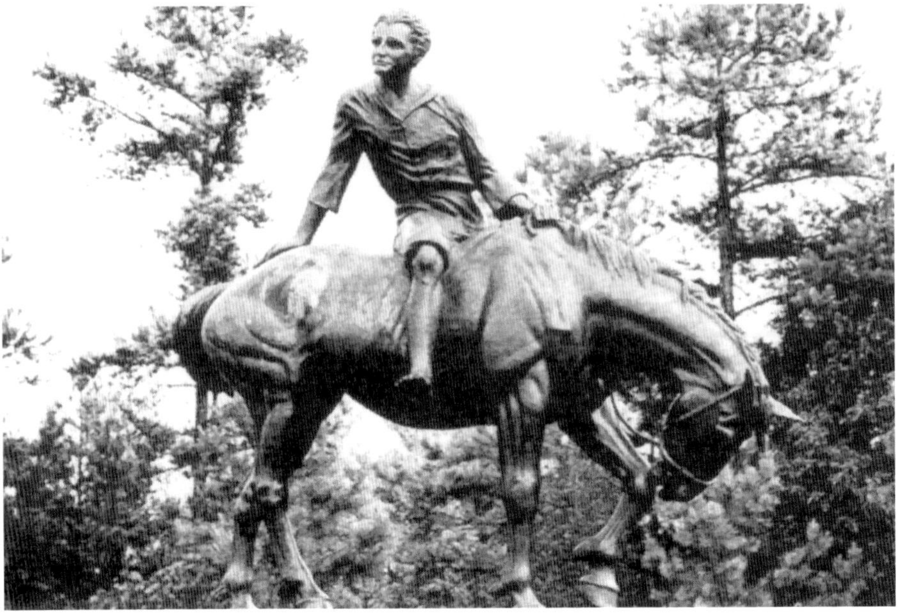

Andrew Jackson sculpture, Waxhaw, South Carolina.

flourished in Ulster all along. The mass of people arriving from Ulster was composed of poor, uneducated folk striving for something of a better life. The Presbyterian Church in Ulster had neither the resources nor the clergy to provide for them. Perhaps also the rather forbidding doctrines (predestination and such) were not what they wanted in a religious perspective of life. They obviously formed and grasped the great popular folk Christianity of the loose-knit "Baptist" congregations and similar gatherings, with their simple theology, local control, inexpensive cost and opportunity for personal fulfillment. From a vague connection to Presbyterianism before they left, many found new roots and purpose on the southern frontier.

The same things apparently happened with the Catholics. Until the early nineteenth century, the Catholic Church in Ireland was illegal, banned and persecuted, and thus had, at best, only a rudimentary presence for the two-thirds of the population whose background was of that faith. In the colonial South, outside the few cities where some of them clustered, those who went inland were attracted to a religious affiliation of the same sort as so many from Ulster. Bishop England of Charleston claimed, in the period from 1820 to 1850, that four-fifths of those who arrived with some kind of Catholic background wandered off into the backcountry and thus were lost to his church. John Carroll, the first Catholic bishop in this country, concluded that most of these people were "name-only Catholics" or had merged into Protestant denominations. Early nineteenth-century missionary priests reported that, due to the lack of a Catholic Church presence, the southern states were full of people who were lost to the old faith. Over and above all, that is the startling finding of one research project that claimed, in 1900, that very few white male Appalachians had any denominational affiliation. What can be added to this claim is the fact that, then and now, most Americans have no church affiliation.[29]

This brings up the matter of the cultural and social distinctiveness of the Scotch-Irish from other people within their area, as well as from those from other parts of the Emerald Isle. The modern designation of "Ulster" refers to six of the original nine counties of that province, with about the full area equally divided along religious lines. The Scotch-Irish champions strived to relegate the Irish aspect to insignificance, while presenting their Ulster as a territory floating off the coast of Scotland, with slight reference to the people "south of the border" in the island land mass as being as alien as Albanians, or perhaps Aborigines. Donald Akenson, who has spent his career examining assumptions about Irish immigration to North America, pulls no punches when he declares, "Ireland formed everyone who lived in it," giving the Irish a high degree of homogeneity. He adds, "They could hate Ireland, love it, hate each other, it matters not. They were of Ireland: hence Irish." He has also established the fact that, of those who have a sense of Irish self-identity, the majority are of some kind of Protestant affiliation for the reasons cited above.

In his excellent study of Ulster emigration, R.J. Dickson does not get into the question of how many of them were Presbyterians and the business of Scotch-Irish; rather, he refers to the migrating people of Ulster as the north Irish. In *The People with No Name*, Patrick Griffin looks at various factions of Presbyterians and other Protestant groups but does not attempt any quantification of them. Additionally, and oddly, he says nothing about the very substantial Catholic population of Ulster (mention does not even appear in the index). Moreover, Ulster at that time remained in contention between the recently settled transplants and those they had dispossessed. Griffin appears to think that none of that seems to matter much, as the people of the British Isles were "busy fashioning themselves as Britons," which was not the case for most Irish people, then or now.[30]

Wandering Irishmen sometimes aroused suspicion. Passing through Virginia in 1753, Patrick Gallahur "inquired the way to Carolina," whereupon he was placed under arrest but managed to escape, leaving behind quite an array of worldly goods for a would-be itinerant: "coats, watch, mare and horse, one buck skin, one coat partly made, one saddle and bridle, four shirts."[31]

Boatloads of people continued to arrive directly from Ireland; 270 Irish immigrants arrived in two ships at Charleston on February 10, 1768. After noting the emigration of English and Scots in this period, Alexander Hewatt commented, "But of all other countries none has furnished the province with so many inhabitants as Ireland. In the northern counties of that kingdom the spirit of emigration seized the people to such a degree it threatened almost a total depopulation." Further, shipping agents finding the bounty equivalent to the expenses of the passage "persuaded the people to embark for Carolina, and often crammed such numbers of them into their ships that they were landed in such a starved condition that numbers of them died before they left Charleston." He went on to account for this exodus:

> *Many causes may be assigned for this spirit of emigration that prevailed so much in Ireland: some, no doubt, emigrated from a natural restlessness of temper, and a desire of roving abroad without any fixed object in view. Others were enticed over by flattering promises from their friends and relations, who had gone before them. But of all other causes of emigration oppression at home was the most powerful and prevalent...Hence it happened that many poor people forsook their native land, and preferred the burning sky and unwholesome climate of Carolina to the Temperate and mild air of their mother country.*[32]

In the few years before the outbreak of the Revolution, there was heavy Irish immigration to the ports of the colonies, and Charleston was no exception. The *South Carolina Gazette* noted the arrival of several shiploads of Irish people in 1772. A Dublin newspaper estimated that in the period from 1772 to 1775, about one thousand Irish arrived at Charleston or Charles Towne, as it was then named. In 1773, a Mr. Hunt advertised in a Dublin newspaper that he had chartered the brig *Hope* for a voyage to South Carolina and was prepared to take passengers, including "young married couples," to settle his lands in South Carolina and Georgia.[33]

As was the case for the majority of people who emigrated in the eighteenth century, most of the Irish came as indentured servants. In 1767, Nathaniel Russell described the arrival of a shipload of Irish servants at Charleston:

> *About six weeks past a ship arriv'd here from Belfast with a number of passengers the owners or merchants there being very anxious to procure as many passengers as possible. Instead of two hundred (Which was the most they could bring with comfort) they brot* [sic] *out 450 & their agreement was for 19 inches room in width for each person but they scarcely had seven, their being so much crowded and the bad usage they met with the master of the ship who cut them off in their allowances of Provis amost* [sic] *three Quarters brot on a distemper which carried off upwards of a hundred on the passage. The survivors were in a most pitifull* [sic] *condition when they arrived here.*[34]

Henry Laurens, who was an agent for providers of indentured servants (as well as African slaves), often decried the treatment of these people. He denounced the cruel usage that "would make your humanity shudder," meted out to a group of Irish who arrived in 1768. His indignation boiled over:

> *I never saw an instance of Cruelty in ten or twelve Years experience in that branch equal to the Cruelty exercised upon those poor Irish…Self Interest prompted the Baptized Heathen in the first case to take care of the wretched* Slaves for a Market, *but no other care was taken of those poor Protestant Christians from Ireland but to deliver as many as possible alive on Shoar upon the cheapest terms, no matter how they fared upon their Voyage nor in what condition they were landed.*

He added, "Compare the pompous tempting advertisements scattered about in Ireland." At the same time, he took a practical business view of the situation, observing the same year, "The Irish Servants have been a great plague to me & I am sorry that they were so put on board the *Wambaw*; they are not worth their homony to me."[35]

The Charleston almshouse often was filled to overflowing with immigrants from the north of Ireland. In 1772, the town authorities dealt with a new influx by hiring wagons to transport 173 of them to the backcountry.[36]

In his study of this trade, Warren B. Smith noted the conditions that existed during periods when the importation of slaves was prohibited: "It was almost as if the British merchants had redirected their vessels from the African coast to the Irish coast, with the white servants coming over in much the same fashion as the African slaves." Another view of the situation is provided by a letter written in Charleston in 1773: "The Irish are considered as welcome Guests as they are generally industrious, and in this low and marshy Country have a Value in being what others deride them for—Bog Trotters."[37]

The *South Carolina Gazette* often had notices about runaway Irish servants. The master of one of them decided to provide a poetic description of the person:

An Irish Mungrel, lately Run away,
When R__ge thought to shew him English play,
But Teague, it seems, did not think fit to stay.
Awake my Muse, in lively Colours paint
A D---l incarnate though he's called a Saint,
A batter'd Beau, puff'd up with haughty pride,
Full of himself, scorns all the World beside,
A hare-brain'd Fop, impertinent and odd,
Whose heaven's his belly, and who back's his God,
A Great conceited Fop, without pretense
To the least grain of Learning, Wit or Sense
Or any thing but Irish Impudence.[38]

In the decade before the Revolution, so many people from Ireland arrived in Charleston that they came to outnumber the German community. During this time, the *South Carolina Gazette* assessed the characteristics of the Irish, Scottish and English people in Charleston. The Irish were "gay, fickle, generous, indolent and pleasure-seeking, the Scots were frugal, strong in adversity, moderate in prosperity and jealous of Scottish honor, while the English shone in superior reasoning, love of liberty and excess in eating and drinking."[39]

Among those Irish immigrants who successfully met the challenges of life in the new country was John Hennessy, who at the age of nineteen arrived in Charleston in 1764 and served for four years as an indentured servant to a carter. He soon acquired his own horses and wagons, and fourteen years after his arrival, he had amassed property worth £4,600, including a brick house, furniture, a gold watch and twelve silver spoons. This achievement was greatly exceeded in the other Carolina by Connor Dowd, who was illiterate but ambitious when he landed in 1754. He began by treading through the countryside selling Irish linen. By 1774, he owned seven thousand acres and other property worth £10,000. For the most part, however, Irish settlers in the Carolinas at least carved out a living, and many failed even at that. That was the common condition of all immigrants in this period.[40]

2

An Irish Revolution

During the American Revolution, South Carolina saw more battles—large and small—than any of the other thirteen new states. The struggle reached a crescendo in the Palmetto State in 1780, when, among the Patriot forces, two-thirds of the fatalities and 90 percent of the casualties occurred there. In 1774, in the prelude to the Revolution, the South Carolina Assembly requested that the governor provide arms to frontiersmen for self-defense, but he refused this request. He did this, according to John C. Miller, because "Tories, Crown Officers and even British regulars, might, in the eyes of Irishmen, be regarded as better game than redskins."[1]

Irishmen and those of Irish roots were prominent in the upheaval in South Carolina. These include the Rutledges, Lynchs, Mannings, O'Neales and Burkes. Two of the four South Carolina signatories of the Declaration of Independence were of Irish stock. Edward Rutledge's father, John (d. 1750), along with his brother Andrew (d. 1755), emigrated from the north of Ireland in 1735. The brothers both served in the colonial assembly. John's two sons were even more eminent. Edward Rutledge (1749–1800) was a representative in the Continental Congress beginning in 1774 and later served in the new state militia. In 1798, he was elected governor.[2]

Edward Rutledge's brother John (1739–1800) was president of South Carolina from 1776 to 1778 and was one of the state signers of the Constitution of 1789.[3]

Then there was the Thomas Lynch family. The first Thomas Lynch (1675–1738) left Ireland, probably from the province of Connacht, as a young boy, became a large plantation owner and served in the colonial assembly. His son, known as Thomas Lynch Sr. (1727–1776), was a member of the Continental Congress and supported the decision for independence, but he died in the spring of 1776. His son, Thomas Lynch Jr. (1749–1779), also a member of the Continental Congress, signed the Declaration of Independence.[4]

Another signatory was Pierce Butler (1744–1822), a native of County Carlow and later South Carolina's first U.S. senator. Butler arrived in the colonies as an officer in the British army. With the advent of the Revolution, he changed allegiances, serving as state adjutant general and as a member of the legislature. Over the course of time, Butler became a wealthy Lowcountry planter. Originally a Federalist, he opposed the Jay Treaty with Britain and the economic program of Alexander Hamilton and soon joined Aedanus Burke as an outspoken supporter of Thomas Jefferson's Republican Party.[5]

Notable figures in the revolutionary Carolinas were the two Burkes, Thomas and Aedanus, both natives of County Galway in Ireland and, if not related, "kissing cousins," friends and correspondents. They were representative of a small but important group of educated Irishmen who were part of the radical and revolutionary movements that spanned the Atlantic in the late eighteenth century. Dr. Thomas Burke was born in 1747 into one of the great families of Galway and studied at Trinity College, Dublin. He first immigrated to Virginia in 1764, where he changed his profession from medicine to law, and after studying law with his kinsman Aedanus Burke, in 1771 he moved to North Carolina. Settling outside of Hillsboro, he named his plantation Tyaquin after the Burke family seat in Galway. A committed democrat, he rose from the revolutionary assembly to the Continental Congress, being first elected in December 1776. In 1781, he was elected governor and rallied opposition to the British invasion of that year. Captured, he was imprisoned at Sullivan's Island in Charleston Harbor, where he renewed his acquaintance with Aedanus Burke, who had also been captured. He managed to escape and renewed his leadership in North Carolina, but due to declining health he did not stand for reelection in 1782. He died the next year at the early age of thirty-six. His brother Redmond, after a shiftless career in North Carolina, became a supporter of the Crown, recrossed the Atlantic and sought compensation for lost property.[6]

Aedanus Burke was born in 1743, also in Galway, Ireland. After study in the seminary of St. Omar in France, he followed the other Burke to Virginia shortly before 1769. Writing to his kinsman that year, Burke clearly demonstrated his awareness of the heritage of his native land. He cited the

> *Antiguity, invincible bravery, benevolence and humanity which distinguished the Native Irish, whilst, that unhappy Country was governed by her own Laws, and enjoyed freedom; tho' from the Scandelous partiality of the English, they are unjustly characterized for Savageness, Cruelty and barbarism.*

Moving to Charleston, South Carolina, he served as an officer in the militia, as judge, as legislator and as chancellor of the state court of equity. After the British occupation of Charleston in 1780, Burke was captured by the British and spent sixteen months in confinement. He managed to escape and returned to military duty. He apparently was on hand to see the surrender of British forces at Yorktown in 1781. He wrote to Arthur Middleton, a Charleston friend, describing the scene of the capitulation:

> *To see these very men who had once reduced us to their power & treated us with cruelty and insult, I am prompted by a Love of Revenge natural to the mind of man and in my opinion, a very justifiable sentiment in a publick* [sic] *war…I detest the British Army, and despise from my Soul the mass of unfeeling men which compose its Officers. But their pride, insolence and insults, their conduct in general in their hour of success, compared with their present situation in which all ranks of them discover a condescention* [sic] *and humility bordering on that of a Spaniel, this, I say, is a good Lesson, & is one instance of the inconstancy of fortune & of the strange Vicissistudes* [sic] *of the Affairs of this World.*

Once the fight had been won, however, he opposed punishment of ordinary Loyalists, although he believed it appropriate to banish the Tory leaders. Rather than allowing the full blast of the pent-up demand for punishment of Loyalists, he delayed the opening of the new state courts. Always a confirmed republican, he attacked the formation of the Society of Cincinnati, composed of officers in the Patriot forces, as a step to the creation of a society based on defined ranks. He vigorously opposed the Constitution of 1789, which he saw, in part, as a British plot. He wrote to a friend:

> *I think it worthy of Observation that not a single instance in So. Carolina of a Man formerly a Tory, or British adherent, who is not loud and zealous for the new Constitution. From the British Consul (who is the most violent*

> *Man I Know for it) down to the British Scavenger, all are boisterous to drive it down…in their efforts to force it on us.*

Despite this, he served as a congressman when the new constitution went into effect. There he opposed any rapprochement with Britain, such as the Jay Treaty of 1793, which he believed originated with "Anglomen." He saw the Aliens Act of 1797 as designed to curb the activities of the foreign born, with the Irish being most prominent. One of his contemporaries, Timothy Ford, was not impressed with Burke: "I found him an arrant Irish man whose conversation though well enough aimed never contained a sentence of good English but on the contrary abounded with blunders, vulgarisms and Hibernianisms." One "Hibernianism" he employed was "Yahoo" to describe a turbulent, irresponsible person, this word straight out of Jonathan Swift's *Gulliver's Travels*. Another person had a different opinion about the judge: "Neither principle nor policy obscured his courage, his Irish wit or his irascible temper."

Another champion of democracy, Burke opposed attempts to legislate social distinctions. A bachelor when he died in 1802, he left most of his estate to the support of Irish immigrants. Historian Robert Calhoon has taken the measure of the man: "It is difficult to imagine any American patriot but one with a background in Irish patriotism connecting the regicides of 1649 [sectarian massacres in Ireland] to the survival of liberty in America in the 1790s."[7]

There were many less prominent Irishmen who supported the Revolution in the state. One of these was Edward McCrady, grandfather of the historian, who emigrated from County Antrim. By turn a teacher, property owner and farmer, McCrady's outspoken support for the rebellion was well known, and when the British occupied Charleston in 1780, he was incarcerated on a prison ship and then banished to St. Augustine, Florida, at that time under British occupation.[8]

Four historians of revolutionary South Carolina had high praise for Irish support of American independence. Dr. David Ramsay (1749–1815), a Charleston physician and politician whose two-volume history of the war, published in 1789, is considered the best initial history of the war, declared:

> *The Irish in America, with few exceptions, were attached to independence. They had fled from oppression in their native country, and could not brook the idea that it should follow them. Their national prepossessions in*

> *favor of liberty were strengthened by their religious opinions. They were Presbyterians, and people of that denomination…were mostly Whigs.*[9]

Another contemporary chronicler, Alexander Garden, a native of Scotland who had direct experience of the Revolution, wrote, "In the ranks of our armies there were many sons of Erin, who felt the injuries heaped upon us as injuries to themselves, and fought for America as they would have fought for Ireland."[10]

The novelist and historian William Gilmore Simms asserted that, alone among the foreign-born groups in Charleston, the Irish opposed continued British rule.[11]

In an 1844 biography of Francis Marion, Simms declared that the members of Marion's famous guerilla unit

> *were sprung generally from Irish parentage. They inherited, in common with all the descendants of the Irish in America, a hearty detestation of the English name and authority. This feeling rendered them excellent patriots and daring soldiers wherever the British lion was the object of hostility.*[12]

In his history of Newberry, South Carolina, published in 1859, John Belton O'Neall, grandson of an Irish immigrant, declared of the Irish, "They had left oppression in their own country and therefore knew the value of liberty. They had long known our enemies, the British, and entertained for them a hereditary hatred…and made more intense by differences of disposition, manners, race and religion." But the O'Nealls were to be found on both sides. Henry O'Neall from the Little River district was a Loyalist whose land was confiscated by the Patriot government, while Hugh O'Neall, from the same area, had his mill burned by Loyalists. In January 1780, Captain William O'Neill proposed launching raiding parties to attack British contingents outside Charleston.[13]

The Revolution began in South Carolina, as elsewhere, in stages, largely driven by events in Boston. Following the first meeting of the Continental Congress in September 1774, in South Carolina a Provincial Congress was elected in 1775. In the wake of the conflict at Lexington and Concord in April 1775, the Provincial Congress formed a compact called the Association to rally support and "to treat non-signers as enemies." It formed a secret committee of the Council of Safety, which dispatched commissioners to generate support in the backcountry. It met with little success among the

German settlers of Orangeburg, Saxe-Gotha and the Dutch Fork. They held land grants from the Crown, were busy with their own affairs and had little political awareness (unlike the rebellious Irish). D.D. Wallace commented, "The Germans in South Carolina generally refused to take part in the revolution, either for or against the government, saying that the king was of German descent, and that they did not understand the dispute."[14]

Many of the Scotch-Irish settlers in the interior were divided on the issue of rebellion. There were those who in protest of a long history of grossly inadequate political representation in the colony violently opposed the movement for independence. Among the leaders of this group were Irishmen Robert and Patrick Cunningham. The state of affairs boiled up into the Battle of Ninety Six in November 1775, in which a Loyalist force was crushed by a large Patriot contingent.[15]

Another element among the Scotch-Irish "hillbillies" was indifferent on the great question of independence, but, declared Russell Weigley, eventually these people "were driven into the rebel's arms by the British policy of studied hostility to the Presbyterian church, based on the exaggerated assumption that religious dissent was synonymous with rebellion." British major James Wemyss, who burned the Presbyterian church at Indiantown, held that all Presbyterian meetinghouses were nothing less than "sedition shops." The Snoddy clan, emigrants from Ulster, were part of the west countrymen who rallied to the side of American freedom. One of them, Captain John Snoddy, who emigrated in 1773, joined in the Patriot cause and, according to family tradition, is portrayed accepting the sword of General Cornwallis (presented by General Charles O'Hara, who had the distinction of surrendering armies to George Washington and Napoleon) at Yorktown in October 1781, probably depicted in a 1783 anonymous engraving rather than in the famous painting (which has Cornwallis on the scene) by John Trumbull. The clan gave its name to a small town in Spartanburg County.[16]

According to Edward McCrady (grandson of an Irish immigrant), the political alignments in Charleston were diverse:

> *The two influential classes in Charleston—the merchants and planters—were opposed to the war. Divided thus on the coast, the whole upper country between the Broad and the Savannah was in open opposition to them* [the Revolutionary party], *while between the Broad and the Catawba the people had taken no part in the movement.*

McCrady makes the point that, rather than leading the revolt, most people in the backcountry, the noted Scotch-Irish, did not get involved in the upheaval in its early stages. It took British and Loyalist incursions there to stir them to anger and violent participation. D.D. Wallace declared that merchants and the Charleston Germans did not support the cause. Patriot leaders "depended largely upon the readiness of the party of the mechanics...to suppress opposition by violence." Irishmen were an element in this group.[17]

There is strong evidence of opposition to independence among the small Scottish population. McCrady declared, "The Scotchmen in Charlestown—especially Scottish merchants, had almost unanimously opposed the Revolution; and so had the many Scottish traders in the Piedmont." Yates Snowden later came to the same conclusion. Apparently due, at least in part, to their need to maintain commercial relations with Britain, Scottish people throughout the thirteen colonies were noted Loyalists.[18]

There was mounting apprehension among Patriot supporters in South Carolina on the matter: Robert Lambert commented, "One ethnic group that aroused fear and suspicion among advocates of American rights was the Scots, who continued and even increased their migration to South Carolina in the 1760s. Mechanics of Scottish nativity were almost constantly suspected of siding with the English point of view." Responding to an attack in a newspaper, one of them declared, "The Day is approaching when every man will be tried. It will then be seen, whether our Class are not determined to be free." Lambert concluded that among Loyalists in the Lowcountry, "their greatest strength lay among a large number of Scots business and professional men and among recently arrived artisans and merchants with close ties to Great Britain."[19]

One indicator of political alignment in the Revolution was the large number of Germans and Scots in the Loyalist militia in the Carolina backcountry. Joseph Johnson related, "On the surrender of Fort Motte, a number of tories were found among the British regulars. Most of these were of German families, who originally settled Amelia township, and built Orangeburg."[20]

William Gilmore Simms also assessed political alignments in the Revolution:

> *The foreign settlers, the greater number of whom had been only a few years in the country, were, with the exception of the Irish, almost wholly opposed to the movement, for any object—they felt no wrong to their interests, they apprehended no danger to their liberties.*

In several of Simms's novels of the revolutionary period, some of his Irish characters were strongly aligned with the Patriot cause. The courageous action of Teddy Macnamara is a good example among many.[21]

The arrival of a large number of Irish people just before the beginning of the Revolution was probably responsible for the revival of the anti-Catholic Pope's Day, which was observed with great hilarity in Charleston in November 1774. Apparently, the holiday was not renewed in the city. During the Siege of Boston the next year, George Washington denounced the custom as ridiculous, childish and offensive, particularly at a time when the Patriot side was seeking to win the support of French Canadians, as well as sustain the small community of Irish Catholics for the Revolution. The landing of two Irish Catholics in Charleston in June 1775, however, set off a stormy response. James Dealy and Laughlin Martin were charged with opposing the actions of the Council of Safety and its secret committee and for allegedly rejoicing in the prospect of arming the Catholics, Negroes and Indians. Revolutionary fervor took hold, and in the first instance of the kind, Dealy and Martin were tarred and feathered, following which "the two unfortunates were carted through the town, and for the first time, people saw the mob at its worst." Dealy was banished, but Martin, "expressing contrition, was allowed to remain."[22]

Patriotic excitement revived traditional animosities, and Catholics became the objects of fear and suspicion. Very few in number, "they were enough," according to Edward McCrady, "in the heated imagination of the Revolutionists to afford something of a Guy Fawkes conspiracy." The petition of Catholic Michael Hubart generated fear that danger was everywhere, "as the times appear to be very troublesome, and numbers of enemies both to the Protestant interest and the present cause, are lurking amongst us."[23]

Attention did not focus merely on potentially subversive Catholics. For shouting "Liberty!" several Negroes were imprisoned. Jerry, a free Negro pilot who owned several slave fishermen, was accused of declaring that if British ships approached Charleston, he would pilot them across the bar. He was hanged and his body burned on August 18, 1775.[24]

Henry Clinton, the British commander in chief in America, was convinced by southern Loyalists that the appearance of British forces in the Carolinas would quickly cause the overturn of Patriot control. David Doyle has pointed out that there was strong Loyalist support among some Irish-born officials in the eastern part of the colony. A coordinated campaign to effect this went wrong from the beginning. A force of Loyalist Scottish Highlanders was

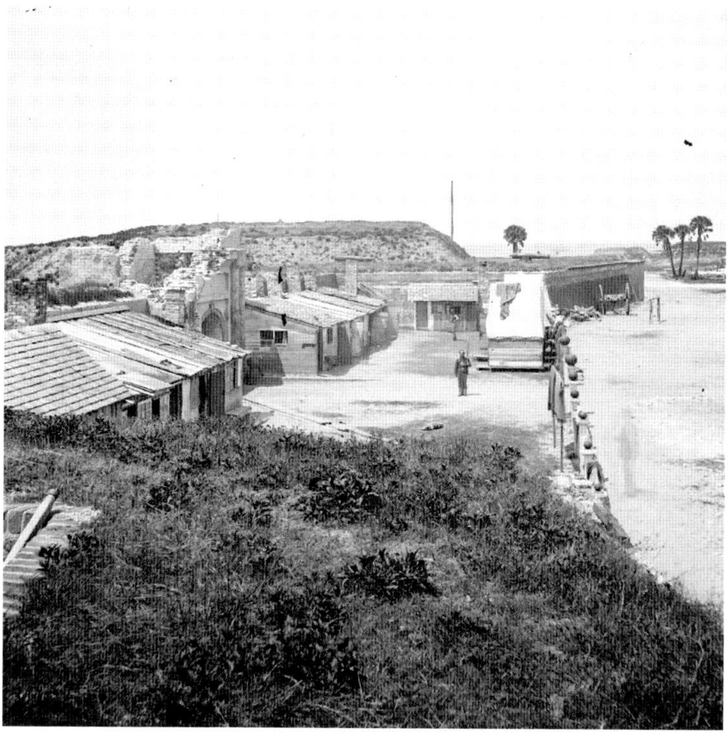

Fort Moultrie, 1865. *Courtesy of the Library of Congress.*

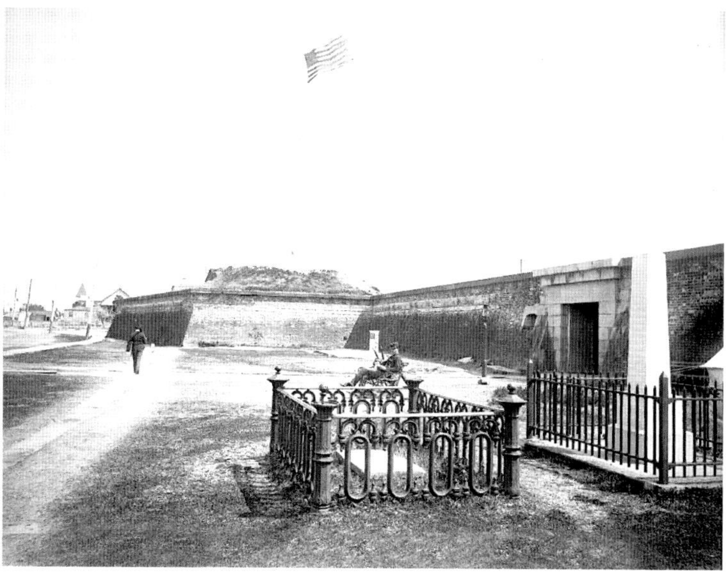

Fort Moultrie, 1900, postcard. *Courtesy of Detroit Photographic Co.*

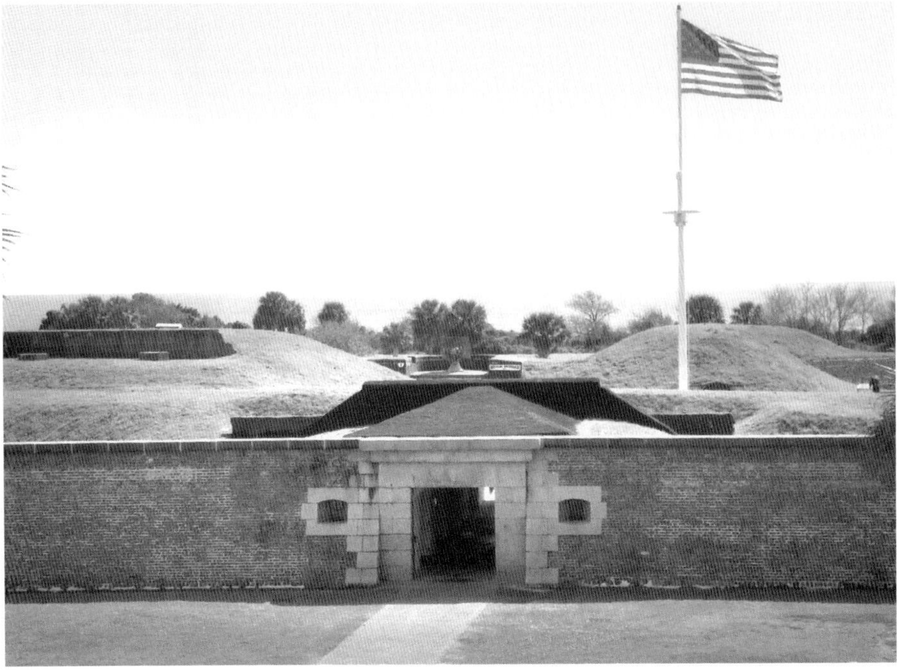

Fort Moultrie, present day. *Courtesy of the National Park Service.*

defeated by Patriot militiamen, led by Colonel James Moore (1737–1777), another descendant of the Irish rebel Rory O'Moore, at Moore's Creek, North Carolina, in February 1776. Over 850 Loyalists, fifteen hundred rifles, a large amount of money and a mass of supplies were captured.[25]

During the British attempt to seize Charleston in June 1776, the Patriot forces resisted at Fort Sullivan (later Moultrie) on Sullivan's Island at the entrance to the harbor. Sergeant William Jasper, who generally is viewed as being Irish, retrieved a fallen standard in the battle and became one of the early heroes of the Revolution. Three years later, he was killed in the Siege of Savannah. A monument to his memory was erected in Charleston. At the beginning of the Civil War, a Jasper Greens company, composed of Charleston Irishmen, was formed and became part of the state militia. The Irish Jasper Greens, a militia group in Savannah, upholds the memory of his heroic deeds.[26]

That neighboring Georgia had an Irish presence in the colonial period is indicated by such place names as Dublin, Limerick, Clare, Ennis, Killarney, Tyrone, Blarney, Cork, Belfast, Newry and Donegal. Irish immigrant

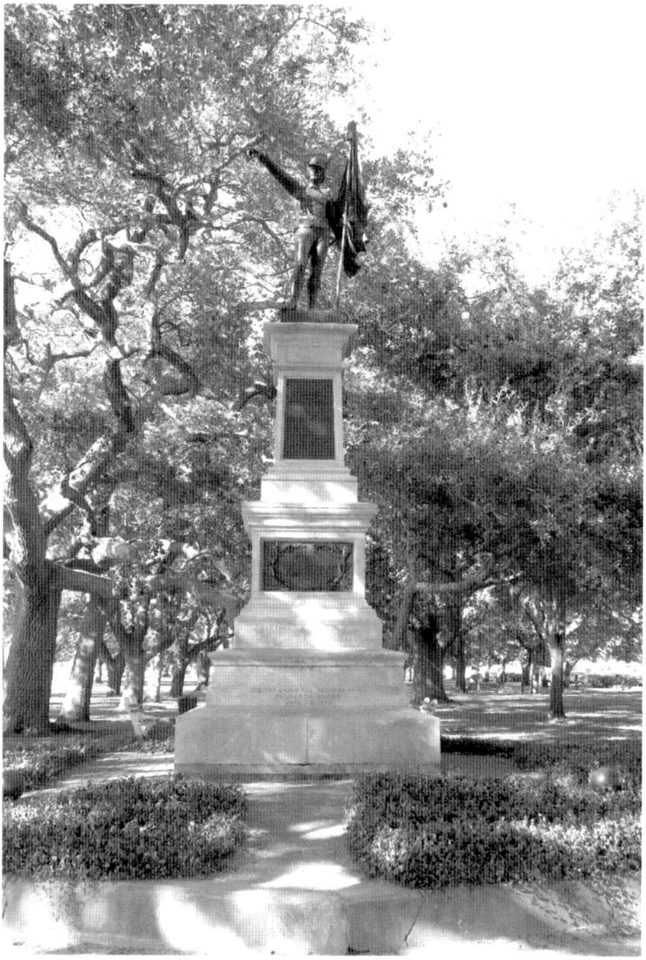

Right: The Sergeant Jasper statue in downtown Charleston. *Courtesy of Julie Scofield.*

Below: A close-up of a quote from Jasper on the bottom of the statue. *Courtesy of Julie Scofield.*

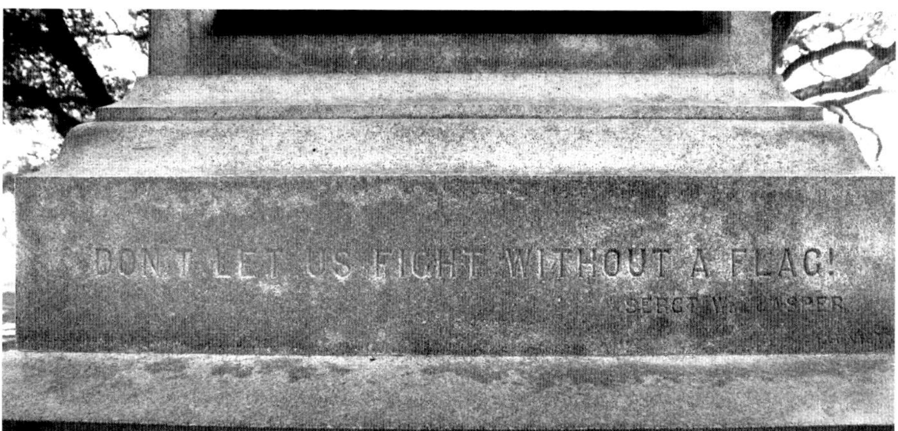

Kennedy O'Brien is credited as being the founder of Augusta, while another named Mitchell laid out the site of Atlanta. The town of Fitzgerald is named after Colonel John Fitzgerald, Revolutionary War commander of horse. The failure of the Patriot-French Siege of Savannah in 1779 meant that the colony remained a Loyalist entity, with Carr's Legion, led by Captain Patrick Carr, becoming known as "the scourge of South Carolina" for its repeated incursions into that region.[27]

General Robert Conway, a participant in the Revolutionary War and a longtime state legislator, donated a large amount of land on which the city of Conway arose. In 1806, he became brigadier of the Sixth South Carolina Brigade. The city was renamed in his honor in 1883.[28]

An Irishman who played a vital role in the Battle of Fort Sullivan was Colonel William Thomson, a native of Maghera, County Derry, and a brother of Charles Thomson, secretary of the Continental Congress, who commanded a force of 780 men that repulsed a much larger British force that was attempting to land on Sullivan's Island. After the British occupation of the city four years later, Thomson was imprisoned.[29]

The place of birth of Edmund Egan is unknown, but with a name like that, it clearly points to Irish origins. "The Rebel Brewer" arrived in Charleston in the early 1760s, claiming to have served an apprenticeship with a London brewer. Together with John Calvert, another supporter of American rights, Egan opened a brewery in 1765. Although civil disruption threatened to bring ruin to his enterprise, Egan vigorously supported the Patriot cause, becoming a member of Charleston's secret committee, organized to rally support for the rebellion, and lent the revolutionary government the substantial amount of £14,000. In 1778, he offered his brew house for sale and turned to building a distillery for the production of whiskey. Egan left Charleston before the British occupation, not returning until 1786, when he again undertook the building of a distillery, an effort that was cut short by his death the next year.[30]

Another forgotten South Carolina Irishman was Cornelius McCarthy, who has been credited with building the first lighthouse on the Atlantic coast at the mouth of the Savannah River in 1759. He is said to have built the first jail in Chatham County, Georgia, and is even credited with being its first inmate. Indicted for sedition at the beginning of the Revolution, McCarthy became a soldier in the Second South Carolina Regiment and served as a scout for Francis Marion (surely with many, many other people). His final notable achievement was to capture twenty-one British soldiers singlehandedly. When asked by his captain how he did this, his reported reply was: "Sure, I surrounded them," but then again, the Irish are noted for their wit.[31]

One of the many people who emigrated from Ulster in the years before the Revolution was William Hill. Born in 1741, he settled in York County, South Carolina, and at the age of twenty-one secured a land grant of one hundred acres. His principal interest was in iron mining and processing, and by 1776 he had acquired five thousand acres, "mainly near Nanny's Mountain, where iron ore was believed inexhaustible." Now that the Revolution had uprooted British authority in that area, the Iron Act of 1760 (which prohibited the production of finished iron products for sale in the colonies) no longer applied, and Hill opened an iron foundry, which produced a wide range of products. During the Revolution, he joined the force led by Thomas Sumter, "the Gamecock." Rising to the rank of colonel, Hill fought in several battles, including that of Rocky Mount, where he was wounded. After independence was achieved, he returned to iron production, now on a much larger scale, and was active in promoting canals and river improvements, transportation being vital to his business. In 1815, he wrote a memoir of his war experiences and died the next year.[32]

St. Patrick's Day was regularly observed in the Continental army (and in the British army), and this included units from South Carolina. On March 16, 1778, the order was issued to the First Regiment of the South Carolina Line that "tomorrow being St. Patrick's Day such Non-Commissioned officers and soldiers as are Natives to the kingdom of Ireland are to be Excused Duty and the paymaster will pay them tomorrow the pay due to them."[33]

From the beginning of the British occupation of Charleston in May 1780, the Scottish Saint Andrews Society continued its activities, with membership extended to some British officers. The news of the victory of Cornwallis was greeted with great celebration. But the gentlemen of the Sons of St. Patrick Society also continued to meet; for their March 17 banquet in 1781, they invited officers of the British army and navy to attend. The Irish Coffee House remained in business, but its proprietor, Abraham Da Costa, a Portuguese Jew, does not appear to have any Irish affiliation. I suppose this was like the modern-day pizza places with no Italian connections.[34]

Almost all military historians agree that the Battle of King's Mountain was a turning point of the war in the South. Here, too, there was an Irish dimension. After the seizure of Charleston in May 1780, that October a British force headed west along the Carolina border hoping to join forces with Loyalist Scottish Highlanders. A formation composed largely of Scotch-Irish, drawn from what were later named Burke County, North Carolina, and Sullivan County, Tennessee, among other places, defeated this force. A British soldier captured at the battle remembered one of his experiences as a prisoner: "Here we heard a Presbyterian sermon, truly adapted to their principles and the times; or rather, stuffed as full of Republicanism as their camp is of horse thieves."[35]

One of the Patriot participants in that battle, James P. Collins, the son of an immigrant from Waterford who was born in York County in 1763, described the aftermath of the battle in a short autobiography:

> *Next morning, which was Sunday, the scene became really distressing; the wives and children of the poor Tories came in, in great numbers. Their husbands, fathers and brothers lay dead in heaps, while others lay wounded or dying; a melancholy sight indeed! while numbers of the survivors were doomed to abide the sentence of a court martial, and several were actually hanged...We proceeded to bury the dead, but it was badly done; they were thrown into convenient piles, and covered with old logs, the bark of old trees, and rocks; yet not so as to secure them from becoming a prey to the beasts of the forest, or vultures of the air; and the wolves became so plenty, that it was dangerous for any one to be out at night, for several miles around; also the hogs of the neighborhood gathered into the place to devour the flesh of men. The local people refused to eat their hogs, "though they were fat" and half the dogs in the area were said to be mad and were put to death. I saw, myself, in passing the place a few weeks after, all parts of the human frame lying scattered in every direction.*[36]

The years did not soften how Collins viewed Loyalists:

> *He was not quarrelsome, but at times, we suppose, from the many conflicts with the enemies of his country, became excited at the mention of the revolutionary war, especially at the mention of the name of Tory, for he had an undying hatred of them.*[37]

Henry Clinton viewed the Irish as "our most serious antagonists." In order to divert opposition from this source, in 1778 in New York, he formed the Volunteers of Ireland, a regiment to be composed of Irish deserters from the Continental army. To command the unit, he appointed Lord Francis

Rawdon, a twenty-seven-year-old Anglo-Irish nobleman. Having risen to the strength of three hundred, the regiment was shipped from New York to South Carolina in 1780. Charles Cornwallis, whose army had just occupied Charleston, dispatched this unit to Waxhaw, on the North Carolina border, in the belief that "as it was an Irish corps it would be received with a better temper by the settlers of that district who were universally Irish and universally disaffected." Instead of gaining recruits, Rawdon found he was losing soldiers to desertion.[38]

Rawdon discovered that he was surrounded by a population who sought "to debauch the minds of my soldiers" and who were succeeding to "a very alarming degree," as well as being "betrayed on every side by the inhabitants." Seeking to stem the tide, he issued a proclamation in which he threatened to flog or ship to the West Indies anyone who had aided a deserter and offered a reward for the return of a deserter: five guineas if the deserter was brought in alive and ten Guineas if only the head was brought in. Banastre Tarleton, another British officer of Irish connection noted for ordering the killing of surrendered Patriot militiamen, recalled the Waxhaw episode, commenting that when Rawdon's force was withdrawn, the local church was burned, probably on the basis that "Presbyterian churches are shops of sedition." As far as Tarleton was concerned, "The Irish were the most averse of all other settlers to the British government in America."

Although Rawdon's threats were not put into practice, Patriot propagandists made great play with this statement. When he left Charleston for England at the end of 1781, he was captured en route by a French ship and became a candidate for execution in retaliation for his refusal to spare Isaac Hayne. British forces soon had a hostage after the capture of Governor Thomas Burke of North Carolina, so Rawdon remained a prisoner until the surrender of Cornwallis at Yorktown, Virginia, on October 19, 1781, an occasion at which he was an observer. After the war, what remained of the Volunteers was shipped to Ireland, and the unit was disbanded in 1784. Back in Ireland, Rawdon, as a member of both the Irish and British House of Lords, denounced the tyranny of the British administration there; sympathized with the United Irishmen organization, which staged the notable rebellion of 1798; and was a strong opponent of the Act of Union of 1800, which combined the two countries into one political entity. So, from an Irish nationalist perspective, Rawdon turned out to be all right in the end.[39]

It was at this time and in this locality that a British soldier inflicted a saber wound on the face of young Andrew Jackson, both of whose parents and two

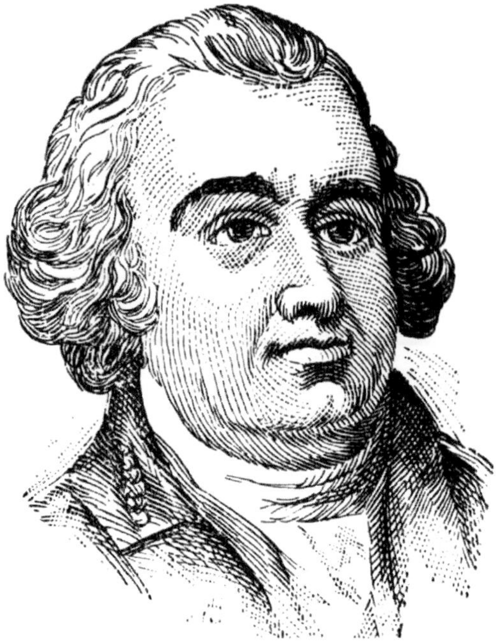

Governor Thomas Burke of North Carolina.

of his brothers were born in the north of Ireland. Old Hickory did not forget either of these matters. He told the Boston Charitable Irish Society in 1833:

> *I have always been proud of my ancestry, and of being descended from that noble race...I am aware...that Irishmen have never been backward in giving their support to the cause of liberty. They have fought...for this country valiantly, and I have no doubt, would fight again if necessary.*[40]

Francis Marion, the "Swamp Fox," is well known to all students of South Carolina history. In his 1844 biography of Marion, William Gilmore Simms declared that there was an important Irish aspect to his exploits in the Revolution:

> *The people of Williamsburg, by whom Marion was summoned from the camp of Gates, were sprung generally from Irish parentage. They inherited, in common with all the descendants of the Irish in America, a hearty detestation of the English name and authority. This feeling rendered them excellent patriots and daring soldiers wherever the British lion was the object of hostility.*

Simms wrote that Marion also secured strong support in the Georgetown, Black River and Great Pee Dee Districts, where many Irish had settled. "The bitter heritage of hate" that these settlers brought with them, Simms continued, "was transmitted with undiminished fervor to their descendants. It was easy to show that the power which had trampled upon the affections of their fathers and tyrannized over their rights in the old world, was aiming at the same object in the case of their children in the new." Simms obviously was not an Anglophile![41]

Historian Yates Snowden has confirmed the strong Irish identity in the Williamsburg area. As a prelude to the Battle of Camden in August 1780, Marion led a small force to Lynch's Creek. "This was the center of the Irish district," Snowden wrote, "which the British had not been able to subdue. The bloody Major Wemyss had attempted it and now Colonel Tarleton was engaged in the same savage errand."[42]

One of the areas of greatest Patriot support in South Carolina, the Chester District, also had a large Irish population. The leading rebel in the area was General Edward Lacey. His biographer, Maurice A. Moore, states:

> *Lacey organized companies and battalions as the fortunes of war demanded and after the manner of partisan leaders, with which he annoyed the Tories greatly, taking many of them prisoners. Of these there were a few in his neighborhood, but not among the Irish. To their eternal honor let it be spoken, none of these York or Chester Irish were Tories, and but few of them took British protection.*

One of Lacey's officers was Captain John McClure, a hero of the Battle of Rocky Mount in 1780. Benson Lossing says that "he was one of the master spirits of South Carolina…and his men were known as the Chester Rock Creek Irish."[43]

According to Bishop John England of Charleston, the involvement of the Irish in the Patriot cause was largely responsible for the eventual removal of religious disabilities imposed on Catholics after the Revolution. Full religious equality did not come quickly. The first constitution of the new state—that of 1778—restricted the office of governor and membership in the legislature to Protestants. In any case, Irish people of South Carolina, as elsewhere, were a powerful factor in the independence movement. In his study of Patriot participants in South Carolina, Bobbie Moss has calculated that these include eleven Lynches, fourteen O'Briens, fifteen O'Neills or

O'Neals, thirty-six Murphys, forty-five Kellys or Kelleys and twenty-two Sullivans. An interesting exercise would be to compare these totals with those of other family names. Patricia Jones has made a lengthy compilation of Irish names in Charleston based on the 1850 census.[44]

Emily Geiger and Dicey Langston are recorded as brave women who carried messages for Patriot forces through British lines, but there was also an Irishwoman (or Scotch-Irish woman, if you prefer) who could be judged a Joan of Arc or Grace O'Malley (Irish sea queen) of the Patriot cause in the Carolinas. Kate Barry (Margaret Catherine Moore, as she was baptized) was the daughter of Charles Moore, a member of the extensive Moore clan in what is now Spartanburg County. According to one source, she was born in Ireland, the eldest of ten children, before her parents emigrated. At the age of fifteen, she was married to Andrew Barry (of the Barrys of Wexford). When the Revolution erupted, Kate more than joined her husband in the struggle for independence. She is credited with successfully acting as a scout for Patriot forces, joining in battle with them in the victory at Cowpens and defying Tory marauders. Not only was she an excellent horsewoman with an intimate knowledge of the backwoods, but she also found time to be the mother of eleven children. Billy Kennedy asserts that "South Carolina folklore about Kate Barry's role in the Revolutionary War abounds and she is remembered as one of the great heroines on the American patriot side." Apparently, her fame did not spread much beyond Spartanburg County, as she is not included in standard histories of the state, but the local chapter of the Daughters of the American Revolution is named after her; a marker at Moore, South Carolina, commemorates her involvement in the Battle of Cowpens; and her family house remains standing.[45]

Robert Lambert has noted that there existed a division in loyalties among the Scotch-Irish in South Carolina. "The number of foreign and American loyalists with north Irish backgrounds," he declared, "suggests that caution should be exercised before accepting a simple 'Scotch-Irish'

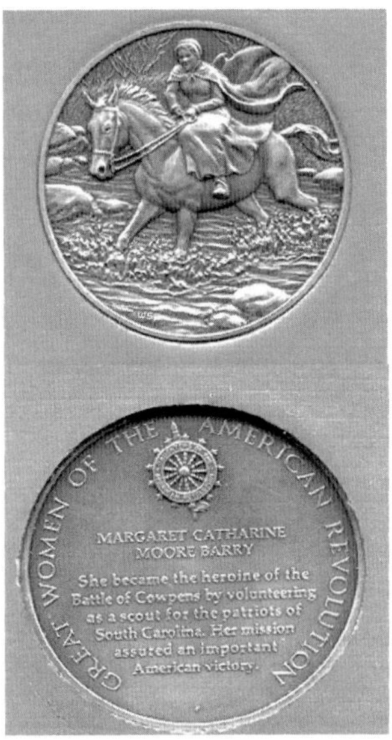

Kate Barry medal. *Courtesy of Tony Chibbaro.*

explanation of backcountry support for independence." Among the very recent immigrants from Ulster to the Lone Cane area, there was strong support for the Loyalist regiment raised there. In the Stevens Creek area south of the Saluda, Scotch-Irish settlers provided many recruits to the Loyalist regiment formed there. To bolster Loyalist support, Major Patrick Ferguson proposed that every Loyalist recruit be promised a farm, which he believed would "at once detach from the Rebels, the common Irish and other Europeans who make the Strength of their armys." Many British observers believed that the whole revolt was due to the anti-Anglican position of Protestant churches, which had, in historian John Shy's words, "persuaded poor Irishmen, who poured into the American colonies in great numbers during the middle third of the eighteenth century, to do most of the dirty business of actual fighting."[46]

One of the Irishmen who remained loyal to the Crown was the aforementioned Robert Cunningham (1739–1813), who arrived from Ireland in 1769 and settled in the Ninety Six District. As a result of his opposition to the revolution, he was imprisoned in Charleston but was released when the British occupied the city in 1780. He served as a brigadier general in the Loyalist militia and after the war went into exile in Nassau.[47]

Another was John Phillips, who was born around 1730 near Ballymena, County Antrim, and emigrated from Ulster in 1770. Taking advantage of South Carolina's offer of free land to frontier settlers, he traveled with his extended family and settled near Winnsboro. Within ten years, with ownership of eight hundred acres, he was a "comfortable back-country farmer." With the outbreak of the Revolution, he led the Jackson's Creek Loyalist militia, which "performed more arduous service for the British than perhaps any loyalist militia unit raised in South Carolina." His political position probably was due to the fact that he was a recent immigrant and may have shared the resentment of some backwoodsmen about the domination exerted by the coastal plantation elite. He became involved in the brutal clashes between contending forces in the backcountry, being accused of being the perpetrator of "many acts of cold bloody cruelty," and justified the execution of a Patriot leader as "a proper example, and Just reward for his treason and infidelity." He had good reason for his position—one of his brothers and two of his sons had been killed in the conflict, with two other sons later dying of fever in the Charleston refugee camps.

After the defeat of British forces and their Loyalist allies, Phillips led a remnant to British lines in Charleston in 1780. Now a colonel in the Tory militia, he was appointed an inspector in charge of providing food, shelter and medical care to the refugees from the Camden District. When the British withdrew from Charleston in December 1782, Phillips was among the many Loyalists who left with them. The South Carolina legislature proceeded to order the confiscation of his property and banished him from the state, with the penalty of death should he attempt to return.

He returned to his native Antrim and, with strong support from Lord Cornwallis, successfully applied for compensation for his losses. Indeed, one-fourth of South Carolina claimants were Irish born, the highest proportion from any former colony. Phillips lived on until 1808, but that was not the end of the Phillips family in the state. One of his sons returned, and his brother James, who never left, was given a pardon and recovered his property, a development caustically noted by former Irish revolutionary John O'Raw.[48]

The first European settler in present Greenville County was Richard Pearis, an Irishman who migrated from Virginia in 1765. Through marriage to a Cherokee woman, he acquired ten square miles of land, where he built a mill and a trading post. As a Loyalist, he was imprisoned in 1776 for nine months. Upon his release, he rose to the rank of colonel in the Loyalist militia. After the war, the British government gave him a grant of land in the Bahamas.[49]

Other Irish-born Loyalists were James and Andrew Moore, of an extended Moore clan, with most of them on the other side. James arrived from Ireland in 1772 and at first supported the Patriot cause, but he was arrested in 1779. When the British occupied Charleston in 1780, he became a cattle buyer for their forces. When the city was evacuated, he went first to Halifax, Nova Scotia, and then to England, where he submitted a claim for losses of £899.

Andrew Moore emigrated from Ireland about 1773 and became a farmer in Ninety Six. After being held as a prisoner of the Whigs for refusing militia duty, Moore joined the British forces in 1780. Like the other Moore, he left with the British evacuation and later settled in County Antrim, most probably the place of his birth. His claim for losses of £905 was dismissed as fraudulent.[50]

There were other Irish-born Loyalists who made claims for substantial amounts of lost property and savings after they left South Carolina. At least two of these had arrived as indentured servants: Michael Reading, who immigrated to Charleston in 1763 and accumulated £695 as a carpenter, and John Hennesy, who acquired a brick house and substantial household goods as a carter. Among those Irish Loyalists who paid their own passage were Thomas Hutchinson, who in a few years built up holdings of 200 acres, "five horses, his chest of tools, twenty bushels of salt, thirteen pairs of cotton cards and debts due to him in the amount of 51 pounds"; William Arters, who made claims for land, cattle, crops and furniture; and Luke Keating, who declared that his loyalty to the Crown had cost him two slaves, 350 acres of land, fourteen cows, numerous hogs and a lot of other things.[51]

Samuel Burke was one of the people caught up in the vortex of the Revolution. Born in Charleston about 1755, he was taken as an infant to County Cork. As a twenty-year-old, he returned to America in 1774 as the personal servant of Montford Browne, who had been appointed governor of the British colony of West Florida. When the Revolution erupted, Patriot forces seized both Burke and Browne, both of whom were imprisoned in Hartford, Connecticut, but were later exchanged for some rebel prisoners. From there, Burke and Browne went to British-held New York City, where they got involved in recruiting Irishmen to join the Volunteers of Ireland; Burke employed "his fluency in the Irish language" for this purpose. Burke became an officer in that or some other British unit that fought in the southern campaign, where he suffered a variety of wounds. Based in Charleston, Burke hoped to acquire some of the land seized by the British in their efforts to stifle the rebellion, but that was not to be. He left Charleston with the British forces in 1782 and in London applied for a pension for his disabilities from wartime service and for compensation for lost possessions in South Carolina.[52]

James O'Fallon (1746–1794), a native of County Roscommon, had a different career in America. After receiving medical training in Edinburgh, he served as a surgeon in the Continental army. Following the war, he established a medical practice in Charleston and in 1783–84 was an instigator of the Charleston Marine Anti-Britannic Society, whose purpose was to oppose leniency for Loyalists and keep British ships out of American ports. John Meleny, in his study of Aedanus Burke, saw O'Fallon as "a known rabble-rouser, in trouble with authority wherever he settled." Having moved to the backcountry in 1785, his petition to form a "Friendly Hibernian Society" was rejected. From there, he moved on to more adventurous pursuits. In 1790, he was appointed general agent of the South Carolina Yazoo Company, where he became involved in a plan to create a separate political entity along the Mississippi. This scheme was squelched by a public proclamation of President George Washington. O'Fallon became an officer in the expedition organized by George Rogers Clark, but he died before the expedition set out.[53]

One of the great figures of Irish nationalist history was Lord Edward Fitzgerald, a generator of the 1798 rebellion. Fitzgerald earlier, however, had been an officer in the British army. Arriving from Cork to Charleston in June 1781, he had a brief military experience in South Carolina, exposed as he was to the "mosquito ridden swamps and creeks of a blazing summer." As an aide-de-camp to Francis Rawdon, Fitzgerald took part in the bloody four-hour Battle of Eutaw Springs in September 1781, where he suffered a bayonet gash to his thigh. He departed Charleston in June 1782 for the West Indies and further adventures.[54]

There was a significant German population in South Carolina, and as a group, they showed no inclination to support the drive for independence. In general, Germans, unlike the Irish, were separated by the barrier of language and had no experience in Anglo-American political traditions, which included frequent forms of elections, agitation and public discourse. Moreover, most of the German settlers were recent arrivals, preoccupied with developing their new property and fearful of the loss of land grants if they rebelled against the king. Efforts made by the Patriot forces in the state to recruit German support were almost entirely unsuccessful.

This is also true of the very small Scottish population, most of whom were involved in business or commerce of some sort and thus did not want to see their economic affairs disrupted by political violence. Their position in this matter marks them at variance with most of the Scottish people who had settled in adjacent Ulster and then moved on to the American colonies—evidence that the formative influence on the Scotch-Irish was their experiences in Ireland.

This sense of being simply Irish was, of course, general appreciation of the early emigrants from Ireland, but this identification has extended to the present. Kerby Miller points out that when people were asked in a 1990 census about their ethnic origins, of the 2.6 million southern whites who responded, 20 percent saw their ethnicity as Irish, while only 4 percent saw it as Scotch-Irish. In South Carolina, the designation "Scotch-Irish" did a little better—7 percent selected this, while 20 percent chose "Irish." About the same result occurred in North Carolina. All of the efforts, claims and bombast of the advocates of the Scotch-Irish thesis from the mid-nineteenth century up to Billy Kennedy (of the *Belfast News Letter*) seemed to have had little success in this regard. Writers of American history books, on the other hand, uncritically did buy into the Scotch-Irish assertion, even going so far as to lump under this heading the likes of John Sullivan,

Thomas Burke and Florence O'Sullivan. Although the research of Michael J. O'Brien resulted in overambitious claims, he did document the presence of large numbers of Irish people from areas other than Ulster who were in eighteenth-century America.[55]

Rory Fitzpatrick, a Dublin-born journalist, in 1989 produced a book in conjunction with a British television program surveying the role of the Scotch-Irish in various parts of the world, in which he decried the efforts of American advocates of the Scotch-Irish identity to assert extravagant claims for that group's importance in the American Revolution. He proceeded to push aside what he saw as the "equally absurd" research of O'Brien, which stressed the great role of the Irish of the other sort in the War for Independence. He moved well beyond historical evidence, however, when he stated that Ulster Presbyterians "supplied about forty percent of the American fighting men." The fact of the matter was that both groups of Irish origins supported the upheaval.[56]

After the British surrender at Yorktown in October 1781, intercommunal violence continued in the backcountry of South Carolina. Finally, with the peace treaty of 1783 came a parting of ways. As many as nine thousand supporters of the Crown left the state. In his study of South Carolina Loyalists, Robert Lambert declares that "Irish Protestants from the interior of South Carolina formed the first distinct group to seek refuge in Britain shortly before and after the evacuation of Charleston." Settled in the Chester area shortly before the Revolution, a group of these people returned to the north of Ireland. The most prominent of them was Chief Justice Thomas Knox Gordon.[57]

For those who remained, there was a need for reconciliation, and it was Aedanus Burke who took the lead in this matter. He not only publicly urged a general amnesty for Loyalists but also, as a judge, released from prison several noted Tories. David Ramsay paid tribute to this

> *Irish gentleman, who, with the gallantry characteristic of his nation, came from the West Indies at the commencement of the revolution to fight for American liberty, generously undertook to advocate the cause of those who, in the hour of danger, had by a change of allegiance sought protection from the present conqueror.*[58]

William Tate played an extraordinary role in the era of the American and French Revolutions. A native of South Carolina, Tate had a

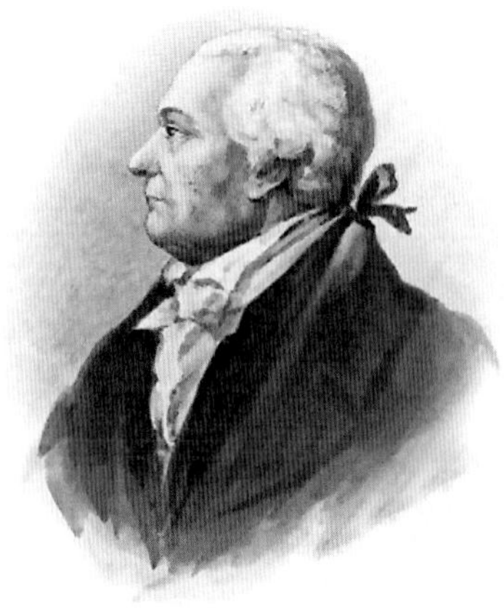

Aedanus Burke.

particular grievance against British rule—members of his family had been killed by Indians who were supporting the British effort to stifle the revolt. Traveling to Europe, Tate became an outspoken supporter of Irish republicanism and, going further, went to France, where he became part of Napoleon's Irish Legion. In an effort to stimulate a rebellion in Wales, Tate became commander of the French force, composed of between twelve hundred and fourteen hundred soldiers, that landed there in February 1797. With no support from any Welsh people, the force surrendered after three days, and Tate surprisingly was not put on trial but was imprisoned for several years. Sent back to France in 1798, he resumed his position in the French army. In 1808, upon the urging of the U.S. ambassador, Tate sailed on a ship due for Charleston and vanished from the historical record.[59]

Revolutionary currents flowed across the Atlantic with the eruption of the French Revolution, which set off controversy between its American supporters, among whom was Aedanus Burke, and its opponents. Archibald Hamilton Rowan, who later was a leader in the United Irishmen organization, came to Charleston due to his connection with Charles Montagu in 1770. His visit was a short one, and he formed a negative attitude toward slavery and the exploitation of Native Americans.[60]

3
In Carolina Life

The first Irish organization to emerge in South Carolina was the Irish Society of Charleston, formed in 1749. Following its first St. Patrick's Day gathering, a poem by Joseph Dumbleton appeared in the *South Carolina Gazette*:

The Muse an Ode select prepares,
With splendid Bowls the Board is crown'd
Thine Harp awakes in solemn Airs
O Saint! while thy great Name goes round,
As Victims on thy festal Day,
Our choicest Firstlings we resign,
And for glad Libation, pay
Our finest Wheat and purest Wine.

This group was probably the forerunner to the Friendly Sons of St. Patrick, which was organized in 1773, with Edward Rutledge as its secretary-treasurer. After the war, probably in reaction to the taint of loyalism attached to the Sons society, in 1786 the Friendly Brothers of Ireland was formed, with Pierce Butler as its president. A branch of the revolutionary American Society of United Irishmen organization was formed in Charleston in the late 1790s.[1]

The 1798 rebellion in Ireland inspired the establishment of the Hibernian Society of Charleston the next year. It is the oldest organization of ethnic origin with its own premises in the country. Its principal purpose was "to

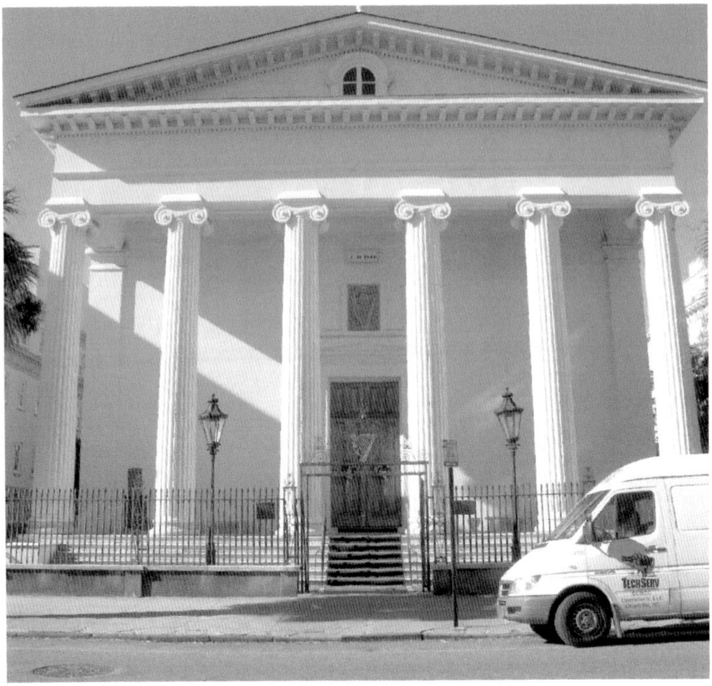

Hibernian Hall, downtown Charleston. *Courtesy of Julie Scofield.*

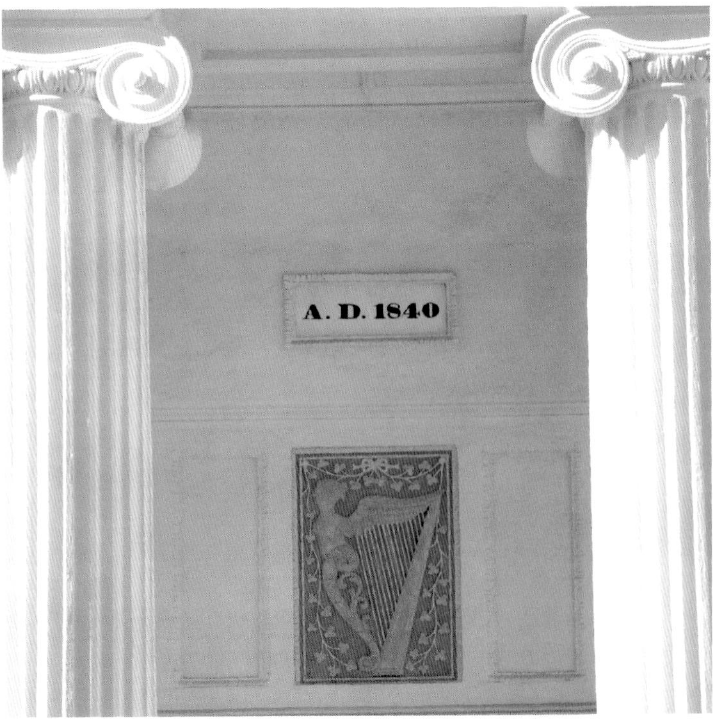

A close-up of the Hibernian crest. *Courtesy of Julie Scofield.*

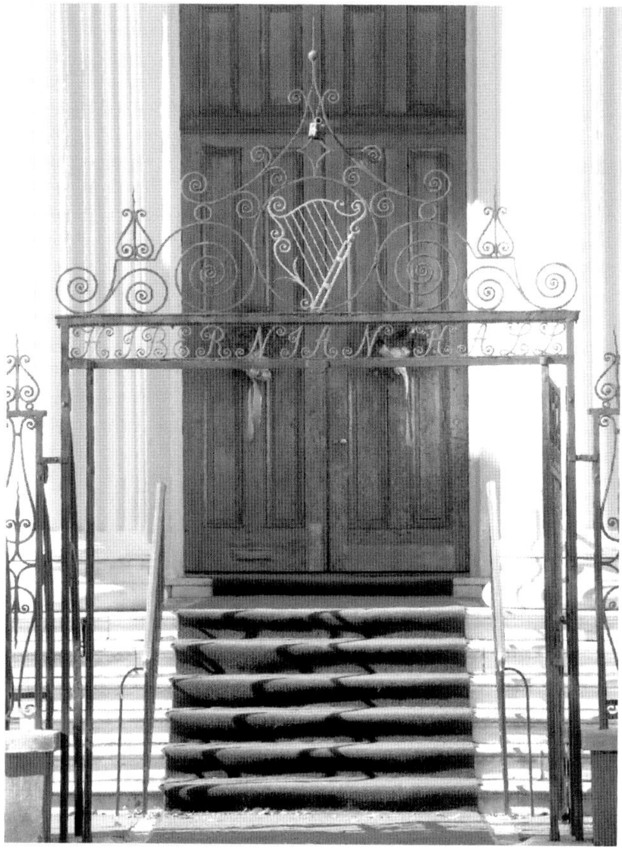

A close-up of the Hibernian Hall gate. *Courtesy of Julie Scofield.*

contribute towards the fund to relieve distressed emigrants." The society proceeded to build an imposing Greek-style meeting hall in the 1840s, and its membership was composed of the leading political, professional and businesspeople of Charleston. Although Irish immigration to the state was small, the society provided financial assistance to just about every Irish person who applied up to the Civil War. In 1830, when James Kenny asked for help toward purchasing a horse, thirty dollars were provided.[2]

There were two other long-established Irish organizations in Charleston. The Irish Volunteers Company of Charleston, formed in 1794, was involved in wars, from the War of 1812 and the Mexican War up to U.S. participation in the European War of 1914–18. It claimed the distinction of being the first company to volunteer for the Confederate army in 1861. The historian Edward McCrady entered the war as a captain in the unit. During the 1850s, leading into the Civil War, there were seven other Irish companies formed in the city: the Meagher Guard (quickly changed to Emerald Light Infantry), the Montgomery Guard, the Emmet Volunteers, the Hibernian Guard, the Sarsfield Light Infantry, the Jasper Greens and the Irish Reserve Company, as well as one in Columbia. After the conflict, the survivors of the other Irish companies apparently merged with the Irish Volunteers. In the 1880s, the Volunteers not only erected a monument to their fallen comrades but also built their own armory on Vanderhorst Street. In the long intervals between military service, the Volunteers Company was essentially a "chowder and marching" group, joining processions on St. Patrick's Day and other occasions. It served as a unit in the U.S. Army during the country's participation in World War I. It remained in existence until about 1929. A revival of the Volunteers, to match a similar organization in Savannah, might be in order.[3]

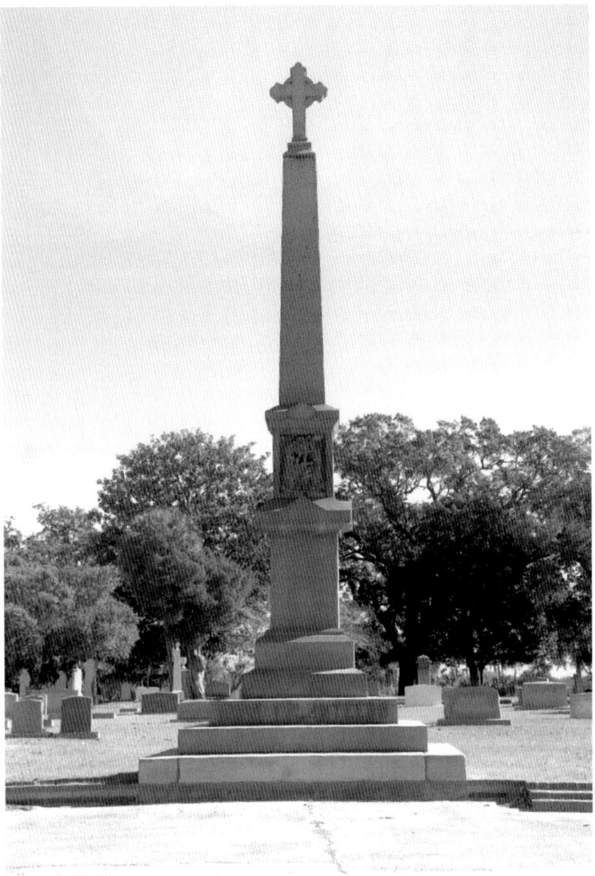

The Celtic Cross Memorial of Irish Volunteers of Charleston, St. Lawrence Cemetery. *Courtesy of Julie Scofield.*

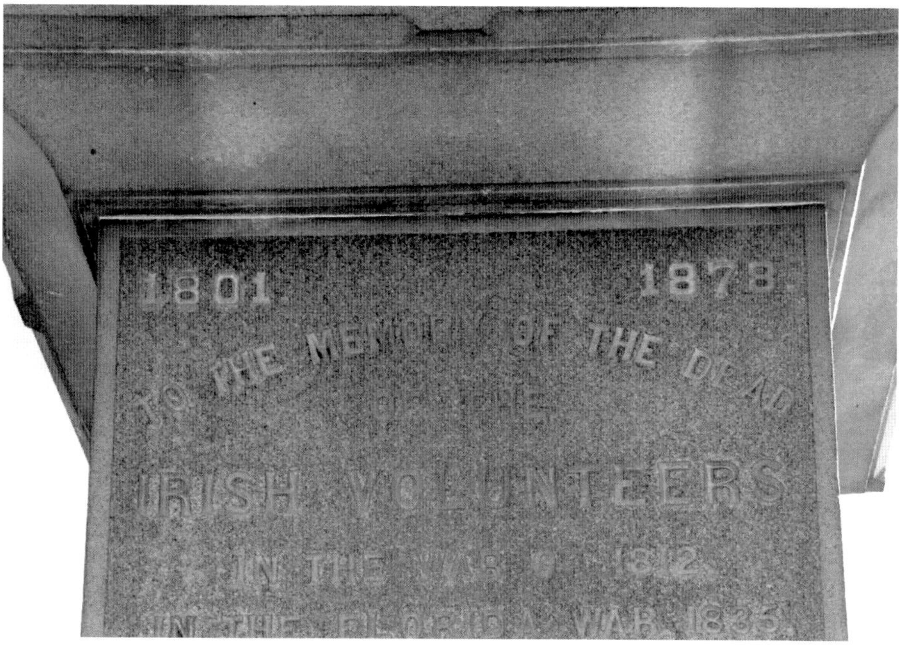

A close-up of the Irish Volunteers plaque. *Courtesy of Julie Scofield.*

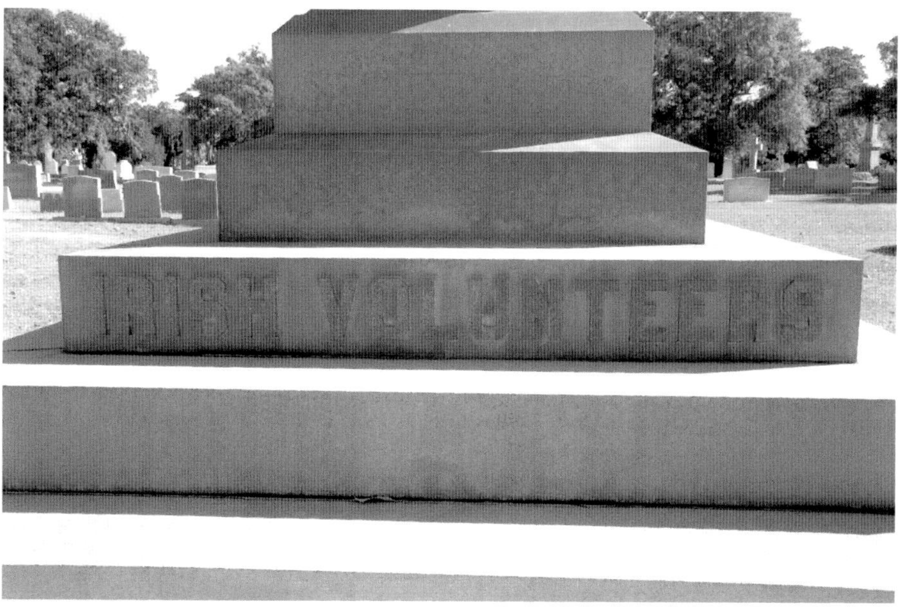

A close-up of the base of the memorial. *Courtesy of Julie Scofield.*

The St. Patrick's Benevolent Society, formed in 1817, for its first thirty-two years was headed by Captain John Magrath, a 1798 refugee, commander of the Charleston Irish Volunteer militia unit in the 1830s and father of a South Carolina governor. At a joint St. Patrick's Day dinner of the three groups in 1841, the guest of honor was the great John C. Calhoun.[4]

As happened in other cities of substantial Irish population, in Charleston there were several organizations formed to further the cause of Irish independence. In 1828, a body was established to support the cause of Catholic emancipation in Ireland, an agitation that generated the first mass democratic movement in Europe and was led by Daniel O'Connell. This was followed by Charleston Irish support for the breaking of the union between Britain and Ireland and, later, the Fenian movement, the Home Rule campaign and others.[5]

Louis Fitzgerald Tasistro, a journalist and would-be actor of Irish and Italian background, arrived in Charleston in 1842 to find that the theater in which he had hoped to perform had just closed; he arrived, he said, "Hibernially speaking, just in time to be too late." During his visit, he found among the merchants that "the greater part are Scotchmen, or the descendants of Scotchmen," yet he also found that there was "a plentiful sprinkling of Irishmen—men distinguished for loftiness of character, and those ennobling qualities of heart and mind which have ever been allowed, by anti-Hibernian writers themselves, to constitute the distinctive features of the Irish character." As evidence of his hugely positive assessment of his own kind, he pointed to the fund provided by Aedanus Burke for assistance to poor Irish people, which he concluded was an "illustration of the characteristic benevolence of the Irish carrying out what Lady Morgan says of them in one of her novels 'that the Irish heart, when tried, shines with redeeming brightness.'"[6]

THE POLITICAL IRISH

It has often been remarked that the Irish have a propensity for politics and government, and that clearly was the case in the first two centuries of the history of South Carolina. The litany of names is a long and, indeed, impressive one. There was Aedanus Burke, lawyer, legislator and judge; O'Brien Smith, born in Ireland about 1756, businessman, soldier and congressman; James Parsons, born in Ireland (probably in Kilkenny), after a long legislative career House Speaker during the Revolution; and Pierce Butler, native of County Carlow, signer of the Constitution of 1789, governor and United States senator. William Aiken (1806–1887), both of whose parents were born in Ireland, was an active member of the Hibernian Society and served as governor from 1844 to 1846. As well, he was president of the South Carolina Railroad Company and is the man for whom the city of Aiken is named. The last governor before the arrival of Union forces in 1865 was Andrew Magrath, son of an Irish revolutionary. The list is liberally sprinkled with Irish names: Noble, Henegan, McSweeney, Manning, Byrnes, Riley. There were two Irish-born governors—Moore and Kyrle—in the colonial period, to be followed by eleven of Irish extraction since 1776. On the local level, the Irish-born Thomas J. Colgan, owner of an iron foundry and gristmill, became a member of the legislature and, during the Civil War, mayor of Sumter.[7]

John C. Calhoun was representative of the Scotch-Irish. Born in the western hill country, he was the son of Patrick Calhoun (1727–1796), who at the age of five emigrated from County Donegal with much of his extended family in 1733. Pat's mother, a brother and several cousins were killed in an Indian attack on the Irish colony of Long Cane in Abbeville County in 1760. John C. Calhoun named one of his sons Patrick after his father. When one of his wife's lady friends reportedly exclaimed, "My good Lord, you have spoiled the child by such a name," Calhoun replied, "If this child lives and becomes as worthy a man as he after whom he has been called, his name will be no disgrace to him." In the period in which he was seeking the presidency, Calhoun joined the Irish Emigrant Society of New York in 1844, upon which occasion he declared, "I have ever taken pride in my Irish descent…As the son of an emigrant, I cheerfully join your Society. Its object does honor to its founders."[8]

The Irish community of Charleston took a lively and influential part in the political life of the city at least since the 1820s. About one-eighth of its citizens were Irish born, with St. Patrick's Day being one of the city's favorite holidays. For most of the period until the 1840s, Charleston had an Irish newspaper—first the *Irishman and Charleston Weekly Register* and then the *Irishman and Southern Democrat* (probably a continuation of the first publication)—which provided a focus to its engrossing political interests. In the late 1820s, many prominent Charlestonians joined with Irish advocates in support of Daniel O'Connell's campaign to gain religious equality for the people of Ireland. Irish causes were given strong support by Henry Laurens

Pinckney, editor of the *Charleston Mercury*, and Irish votes helped Pinckney gain control of the city government.[9]

During the nullification crisis of 1832, Calhoun squared off with another Carolina native of Irish stock—President Andrew Jackson. The Irish Volunteers of Charleston militia company held a meeting to address the controversy. Despite the plea of Bishop John England to remain faithful to the Union, the company voted to support nullification, action that later drew the comment of F.M. Salley, "They were for the State first, last and all the time. And what else could we expect? How often do you find an Irishman wrong in politics, or possessing a bad idea about what constitutes liberty?" Yet the *Irishman and Southern Democrat* strongly opposed nullification. Among those who rejected nullification was Judge John Belton O'Neall. In the 1850s, opponents claimed that the Irish control of the police force was an important factor in municipal elections.[10]

Early Lace-Curtain Irish

James Hoban, the Irish-born architect who designed the White House, only spent a few years in Charleston but was in charge of the design of the first statehouse in Columbia. A native of Callan, County Kilkenny, Hoban studied architecture in Dublin and became "universally acquainted with men in the building line in Ireland." He immigrated in 1785, first to Philadelphia and then to Charleston. He spent five years in the latter city and designed a number of buildings, including the notable building at the corner of Meeting and Broad Streets, now a courthouse. He left South Carolina in 1792 with a letter of introduction from Henry Laurens and Aedanus Burke.

The project of building a president's house in the nation's capital had been mired in controversy and delay. He traveled to Philadelphia and had several meetings with President Washington. In 1792, Washington announced that Hoban had won the competition for the building. Irish political influence in public construction projects obviously goes back a long way. Hoban not only designed the White House, supposedly borrowing the model of Leinster House in Dublin (since 1922 the site of the Irish parliament), but he was also in charge of rebuilding the "presidential mansion" after it was burned by the British in 1814. During the course of the original construction, he met with Washington at Mount Vernon, and the building was completed in 1798. The British minister in Washington was not pleased by this development:

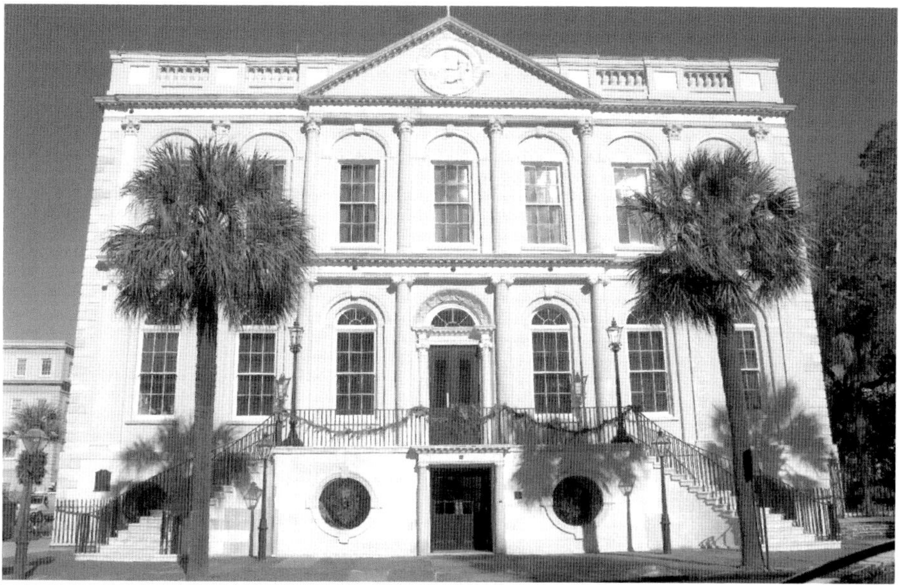

Charleston City Hall. *Courtesy of Julie Scofield.*

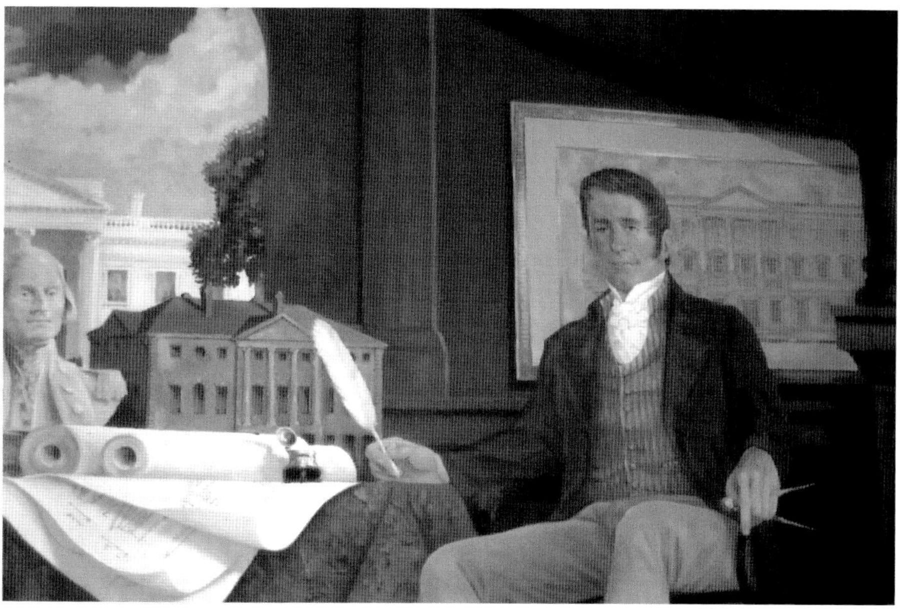

James Hoban, architect of the White House. *Photo by Jessica Fowler. Portrait owned by the James Hoban Society of Charleston and reproduced here with permission.*

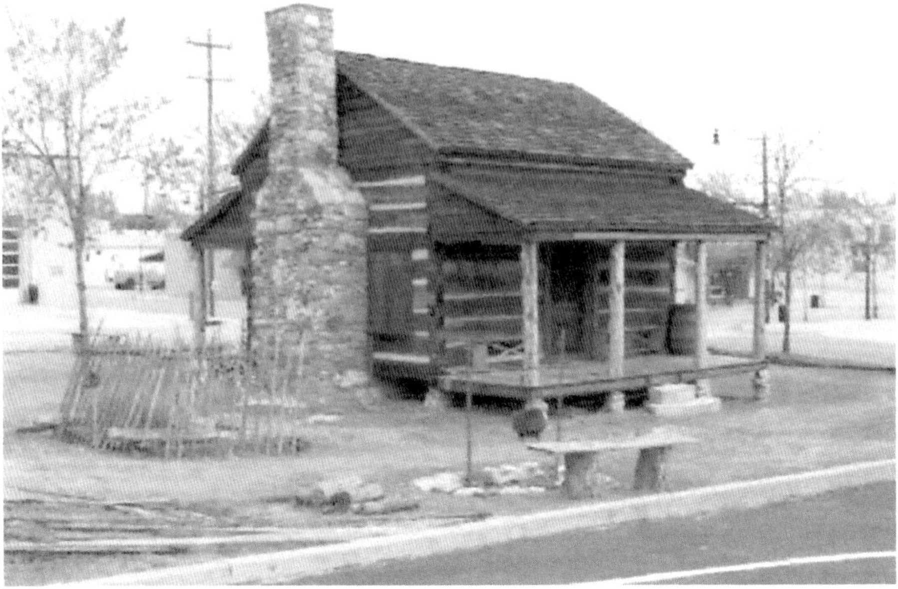

Michael Gaffney House, Gaffney, South Carolina.

> *The President's house was erected by an Irish mason who gave as his own the plan the Duke of Leinster's house in Dublin, which being shewn* [sic] *to General Washington was approved of by him, and the Irishman who had been but a journeyman under the real architect and designer of the plan, was appointed to supervise the building. He left out the upper story, however, and built no cellars.*

Due to Hoban's involvement in the design and construction of many government buildings, it has been said of him that "Hoban was the personage connected with the Federal City who remained continuously identified with it from its inception." Having fathered ten children, acquired much property and served as an officer in the Washington Artillery and as a member of the city council, he died in 1831. A James Hoban Society was formed in Charleston in 2002.[11]

Michael Gaffney (1775–1854) left his native Granard, County Longford, in 1797, probably as a result of British attempts to quell opposition that exploded into rebellion the next year. After sojourns in New York and Charleston, he traveled westward to the foothills of the Appalachians. There he established a tavern, store and guesthouse at what became known as Gaffney's Crossing. Eventually, he acquired a large amount of land and carried on farming with the help of fifteen slaves. In the period of rising tension with Britain leading up to the War of 1812, Gaffney organized a militia company, of which he became captain in 1808. There was exceptional opposition to Britain in the backcountry due to the fact that "a large number of recent settlers of the area had fled Ireland to escape imprisonment by the British for their activities in the Great Rebellion."[12]

A leading figure in the intellectual life of Charleston in this period was the Irish-born priest Dr. Simon Gallagher (1756–1825). He was not only pastor of the first Catholic parish in the state, St. Mary's, but also, beginning in the early 1790s, a faculty member in the College of Charleston, teaching courses in logic, mathematics, natural philosophy and astronomy. In 1811, he became the first chairman of the Charleston Board of School Commissioners. He later came into dispute with Bishop England, as well as with some of his parishioners, but the conflict was eventually resolved.[13]

Another Irish-born priest, James Wallace, was born in Kilkenny about 1783 and educated at Maynooth Seminary. After his arrival in this country in 1817, he attended Georgetown University, following which he became a member of the Jesuit Order. He played an important role in the intellectual development of South Carolina College in the early years of the nineteenth century. The only Catholic faculty member in that period, he was a professor of mathematics from 1820 to 1834; he also had a strong interest in astronomy. With the growth of Protestant fundamentalism, he was removed from his position, along with several other faculty members. By this time, he had acquired considerable property—three houses in Columbia, an island in the Congaree River and a strip of land along the canal (later the site of the state prison), as well as some slaves, of whom "the most valuable escaped to the Free States after his death." When he died in 1851, he left his wealth for the establishment of a boys' orphan asylum in Charleston.[14]

Michael Tuomey (1805–1857), a native of Cork, traveled to America in the late 1820s and studied at Van Rensselaer Polytechnic Institute. Appointed state geologist of South Carolina in 1844, he was the author of pioneering works on South Carolina geology and fossils. A longtime participant in the geological survey of the state, in 1848 he produced a "Report on the Geology of South Carolina," which D.D. Wallace declared to be "one of the two outstanding works on the subject." He later became professor of geology at the University of Alabama. Together with F.S. Holmes, in 1857 he published *Pleistocene Fossils of South Carolina*.[15]

John England was an important person both in South Carolina and in the Catholic Church in early nineteenth-century America. Born in Cork City in 1786, he was appointed bishop of Charleston in 1820 at the age of thirty-four for a diocese that covered both South Carolina and Georgia. From the beginning of his mission in South Carolina, England set out to divorce his position from the traditions of the Catholic Church in southern Europe regarding the Inquisition and suppression of divergent views concerning Christian doctrine. In a ringing declaration, he upheld freedom of religion: "I profess in America what I professed in Ireland, and what they who were my associates in Ireland still profess." He quickly grasped that experiences in Ireland equipped Irish emigrants to deal effectively with the social and political realities they found in the New World: "The Irish are easily amalgamated with the Americans. Their principles, their dispositions, their politics, their notion of government, their language and their appearance become American very quickly."[16]

While expanding the structure and membership of his church, England established both a nonsectarian classical academy and a Catholic seminary. Although Charleston was not to be an important center of Irish immigration, and the Catholic Church thus only grew to modest proportions, England was prolific as both a spokesman for his religion and for Irish concerns. Established in 1822, his *United States Catholic Miscellany* was the first long-lasting Catholic newspaper in the country and a major forum for a wide variety of public affairs. He opened a school for free blacks, but southern opposition to abolitionism soon reared its head. In 1835, after a Charleston mob burned abolitionist printed matter at the local post office, it marched on the Catholic compound to attack the black school. Irishmen in the city militia put a halt to that, but England agreed to close the school provided other churches in the city end their educational efforts for black people. The matter of slavery again reared its ugly head in a very public way in 1842. In a sweeping condemnation of the slave system, Daniel O'Connell declared, "Over the broad Atlantic I pour forth my voice, saying, come out of such a land, you Irishmen; or if you remain and dare to countenance the system of slavery that is supported there, we will recognize you as Irishmen no longer."

England, who was a friend of O'Connell, made the principal reply. He charged that O'Connell had assumed the Irish in this country were "heartless wretches [because] we cannot at once do all that your imagination conceive to be perfection, and which we who have the experimental knowledge have irrefragable evidence to be destructive folly." He concluded by hoping "that you may succeed in raising the ruined population of Ireland to the level of the comfort of the Carolina slave." But he returned to the matter of slavery in his final literary effort, "Letters on Domestic Slavery." He had often been asked if "I am friendly to the existence or continuation of slavery. I am not—but I also see the impossibility of now abolishing it here. When it can and ought to be abolished is a question for the legislature and not for me."[17]

Even before Charleston confronted the break in American unity, the Catholic Church suffered a great loss when its cathedral burned down in the great fire of December 1860. This also marked the end of England's Catholic newspaper. Despite the efforts of Bishop Patrick Lynch, with emancipation after the Civil War many blacks left their connection with the church to establish their own congregations, although some remained in the Catholic fold.[18]

Jeremiah O'Connell (1821–1894) was one of three Irish-born brothers who all became priests and held the fort for Catholicism in Columbia and westward from the 1840s. A doctor of theology, he served as pastor of St. Peter's parish from 1848 until 1871. Not a man to run from controversy, he displayed enormous energy and dedication, leaving a vivid, if convoluted, account of those efforts in his remarkable *Catholicity in the Carolinas and Georgia*, which was published in 1879.[19]

Although not as eminent as many other Irishmen in the state, the life and times of John O'Raw is documented in the series of letters he wrote to his family in Ireland. O'Raw was born in a Catholic family of merchants and farmers near Ballymena, County Antrim, in 1783. A participant in the 1798 rebellion, he was sentenced to be hanged but escaped and remained in his native area until his emigration in 1806. In Charleston, he was taken under the wing of his relatives in the O'Hara family, established as merchants in the city beginning in the 1770s. He did not remain in the city long. He soon returned and, after serving in the navy in the War of 1812, became a member of the Hibernian Society. He eventually owned a grocery store on Meeting Street. As a communicant of St. Mary's Catholic Church, in the period from 1815 to 1819, O'Raw became one of the leading opponents of the appointment of a conservative French priest to the parish. Probably for business and family reasons, O'Raw returned to Ireland in the late 1820s, thus becoming one of the few Irish immigrants to make the return circuit. He died in 1841.[20]

The O'Hara family surely was an industrious clan. In the 1780s, Daniel O'Hara was an agent for ships between Larne in Ireland and Charleston.

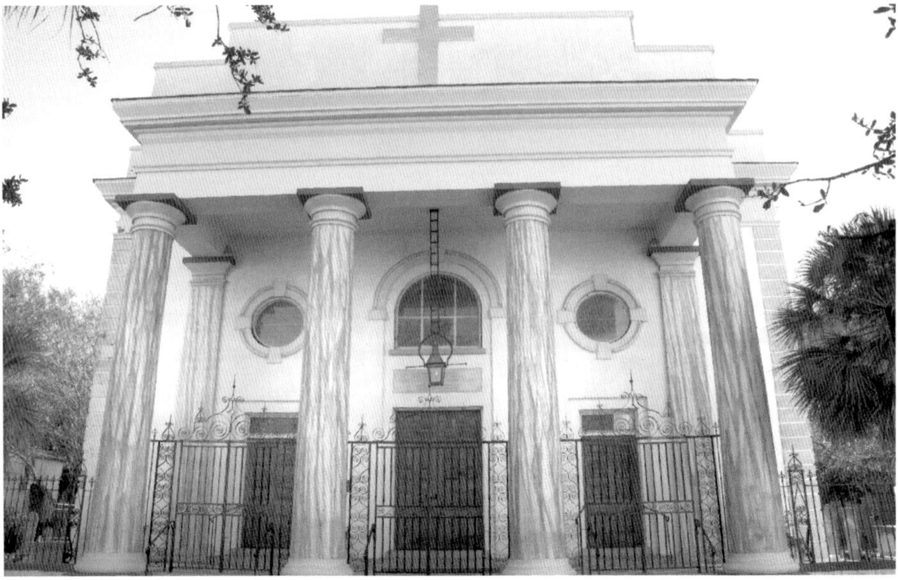

St. Mary's Church, downtown Charleston. *Courtesy of Julie Scofield.*

The *Irish Volunteer* vessel regularly made this circuit in the late 1780s and early 1790s.[21]

A second William Hill is part of the story of Ulster migration to South Carolina, this one living through a whole span of history in the Palmetto State. Born in 1805 in County Antrim to a Presbyterian family that supported the 1798 rebellion, Hill immigrated to America in 1822, settling in the Abbeyville District. Although he was strongly attached to the libertarian principles of the United Irishmen, he only slowly got involved in American political life, becoming a citizen twelve years after his arrival. His fortunes slowly rose as he became a farmer, slave owner, merchant and ironmonger. Public esteem rewarded him with the position of local judge beginning in 1852.

Hill's southern circumstances began to separate him from his Irish loyalties. Although he named one of his sons Robert Emmet, after the Irish revolutionary, he took strong exception to Daniel O'Connell's denunciation of slavery. When famine-era Irishmen began to arrive in the state, Hill was stunned by what he viewed as the "poverty and want, rags, squalor, and wretchedness" of many of them. These were, he said, "the *real* Irish, of papist stock." His Irish affinity was further tested in the face of Confederate defeat, which he attributed to "tens of thousands" of Irishmen in the Union army who had crushed "a people struggling for self-government regardless of anything but their filthy pay." On top of that, he was appalled by the behavior of Irish Union soldiers stationed in Abbeville, who, he observed, "mingle with the Negroes with as much affinity as if of the same blood." A brief return to Ireland in 1867 apparently did not restore his previous political ideals.[22]

Christopher Fitzsimmons got involved in a wide range of activities. Born in Ireland in 1762, in Charleston he became, in turn, a merchant, brewer, importer of slaves, planter and commissioner of the Bank of South Carolina. He carried on these varied business activities until his death in 1825.[23]

By this period, Charleston had a sizeable Irish population. A substantial number of them were temporary residents—arriving in the autumn and departing (usually to New York City) before the summer heat. Based on the 1850 U.S. census, Margaret Motes has estimated that there were four thousand Irish-born people in South Carolina, twenty-four hundred of whom lived in Charleston. In his study of antebellum South Carolina, Rosser H. Taylor declares:

> *Among the non-English elements in Charleston, the Irish were the most turbulent and pugnacious. There were a great many Irishmen in Charleston who, true to Irish form, drank whiskey freely and fought with or without provocation. Jacob Schirmir mentions several disturbances created by the Irish, of which the following is somewhat typical: "Fight this afternoon as the boat was leaving the Island. A row took place near the boat between some young men and the Irish when Scott and Carter were considerably cut up."*[24]

As in other places, Irish people gradually worked their way up. They created competition with free blacks for jobs as carters and dockers. As happened throughout urban America, many Irishmen sought the security and influence found in fire and police departments. According to local legend, the first Irish policeman in Charleston was Timothy Patrick Murphy. On one occasion, when a horse fell dead on Vanderhorst Street, Officer Murphy was sent to deal with the matter and write a report. He proceeded to drag the horse around to Meeting Street. Asked why he did this, Tim replied that he did not know how to spell Vanderhorst. By 1860, Irishmen were a majority in the Charleston police force. "Pat the cop" was a familiar figure in almost all American cities in the late nineteenth century. At first, Paddy was put in the police wagon and then put others in it. Dwight Eisenhower from Kansas knew that a *shemus* referred to an Irish detective.[25]

The principal activity of Irishmen in the first half of the nineteenth century, of course, was to provide labor for building the first canals and then railroads, as well as a range of public buildings. Their skill as stonecutters provided the labor for the latter work, with their greatest accomplishments including building the new statehouse in Columbia and the customhouse in Charleston. In canal building, beginning in the 1820s, they not only built the Columbia Canal and the Santee Canal but also six others in the state. They found a ready market for their labor in railroad building, starting with the Charleston to Hamburg line beginning in the 1830s. In his study of labor conditions in South Carolina in the antebellum period, Richard Morris comments, "Most conservative of the slave states, South Carolina permitted long-established attitudes towards the control of Negro labor to condition her relations with the numerically smaller, but nonetheless significant, group of white workers, skilled and unskilled." This attitude was manifested in a response in 1855, when Irish construction workers building the Northeastern line went on strike seeking to increase their wages from $1.00 a day to $1.25. Twenty-three of the strike leaders were convicted of activity "directed to an unlawful end" and were fined $5.00 each and sentenced to two months' imprisonment. In imposing sentence, Judge Withers allowed that

> *your native Ireland has contributed a rich contingent to the best blood of mankind…Its bone and muscle have subdued the wilderness and made it "blossom as the rose,"* [but the] *Emerald Isle has likewise afforded us the most troublesome specimens of humankind.* [Further,] *a great proposition of those we receive in Charleston from Ireland manifest a proclivity to turbulence.*[26]

The doctoral thesis of Dee Dee Joyce of the College of Charleston on the role of Irish workers in Charleston in the antebellum period provides a wealth of material on their wide-ranging activities.[27]

John O'Raw may not have been a notable Irish immigrant in Charleston, but his life there is recorded in letters he sent to his family in Ireland. He was born in the politically mixed town of Ballymena in County Antrim in 1873. From a Catholic family in an area largely made up of Scottish Presbyterians, O'Raw, although only fifteen years of age, took part in the 1798 rebellion and fought in the Battle of Antrim Town, led by Henry Joy McCracken. Sentenced to hang, he escaped and, through the intersession of his loyalist father, remained free until his immigration to America. In 1806, he arrived in Charleston, where he already had kinsmen and friends. Almost immediately he got employment with Charles and Henry O'Hara, whose family had been in the city since the 1770s and were merchants on Broad Street. Charles was a member of the Hibernian Society, which was founded to aid Irish refugees from the 1798 uprising. He did not remain in that job for long, as "I thought it prudent to leave Charleston as it commonly proves fatal to Europeans to Stay here the first summer after coming in." After traveling around (and surviving a four-month-long illness), he became a teacher for a year in the midlands, boarding with a sister of a family from the Ballymena area. There he encountered a fellow Ulster man: "Johnny Boyd has bought 130 acres of land for 300 dollars…He is very contented and happy…He has made a good change…He will in a Short time be Rich which he never would have been in Ireland." Back in Charleston, he met up with one of his kinsmen, Alexander O'Hara of Belfast, to whom O'Raw loaned some money without repayment. As a consequence, "He was afterwards in a poor Situation in this City Borrowing from every person he could get from & at last put in Jail for his Boarding. He is now back some where in the Country."

At this point, apparently O'Raw returned to work for the O'Hara brothers and was listed in the city directories as a grocer's clerk in 1812. Having served in the war of that year and becoming a U.S. citizen in 1815, O'Raw's condition improved, as now he had his own grocery on Meeting Street, which status obviously afforded him membership in the Hibernian Society. He was one of the Irishmen who, in 1815, refused to acknowledge the appointment as priest to the city's Catholic church a French clergyman, not because of any ethnic consideration but "due to his outspoken animosity towards the radical principles for which they and their Protestant countrymen had fought in Ireland." He never married while in Charleston but owned two slaves. For reasons unknown, he returned to his family in County Antrim about 1829 and died in 1841. Although his outward voyage had been horrific, he was one of the few Irish people to make a return passage across the Atlantic.[28]

Sons of Irish parents emerged into influential positions in Carolina life. One of these was Bartholomew Carroll, who edited a literary journal and wrote widely on the history of the state, as well as a general history of the country. In 1838, he delivered a St. Patrick's Day oration to the St. Patrick Benevolent Society and the Irish Volunteers. Ten years later, he affirmed his Irish identity in a stirring speech to the Association of Friends of Irish Independence, also in Charleston.[29]

Henry Conner, born of Irish parents in 1797 in Mecklenburg County, North Carolina, rose to be a prominent Charleston businessman in the antebellum period. He was one of the organizers of the Bank of Charleston and president of the South Carolina Railroad in 1850. A strong supporter of states' rights, he was a signatory to the Ordinance of Secession in December 1860. Additionally, he had a strong Irish attachment. He served as chairman of the Hibernian Society's famine relief committee and became president of the society later that year. Establishing something of a family dynasty in the organization, his son, General James Conner, was president from 1871 to 1874, to be followed by his grandson, Henry W. Conner, from 1913 to 1915 and, finally, his great-grandson, James Conner, from 1937 to 1939.[30]

IRISH AND CATHOLIC

When he became the first Catholic bishop in the South, John England began the process of building a lasting foundation for his denomination. An immediate issue, widespread in the new nation, dealt with trusteeism—the demand by many Catholic laymen that the church members, not the clergy, should direct and control affairs of the local parish. Using his notable diplomatic skills, England managed to overcome this opposition to clerical control by establishing councils of laity to observe and advise on church affairs, although actual authority remained with the hierarchy.[31]

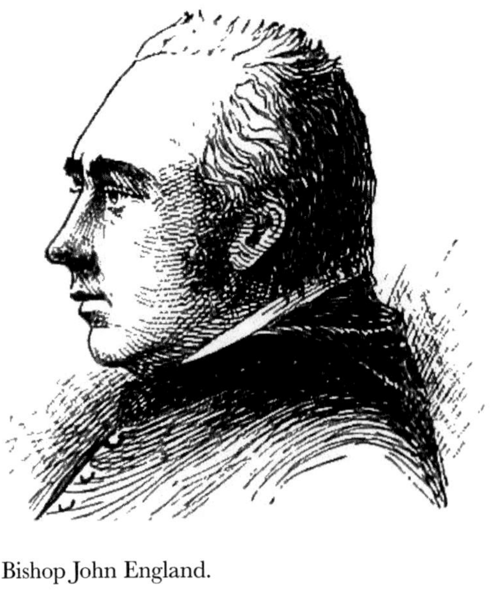

Bishop John England.

By the 1820s, a small Irish community grew in Columbia, the state capital, with the influx of laborers, stonecutters and masons to work on the new capital building, designed by James Hoban of Dublin, and the Columbia Canal. A Catholic presence in the city is seen in the establishment of St. Peter's Catholic Church in 1821. According to Jeremiah O'Connell, the canal diggers "were nominally Catholics, but scarcely a half dozen practiced their religion or entered the church except on some semi-religious occasion, such as a wedding or a funeral. Of no advantage to the Church in any sense, they were, on the contrary, factious and censorious, and an exception to anybody of Irish Catholics with whom I ever came into ministerial relations." The Hibernian Benevolent Society, founded in 1851, was not for the likes of the roughneck canal diggers. Although immigrants were a very small part of the population of the city, the Irish were the largest group.[32]

By the 1840s, the congregation numbered about one hundred. Dr. O'Connell related, "They were generally poor Irish people and gained their support by conducting retail stores or services in the Asylum." Moreover, "At one time we had Mass in the jail on Sundays as regularly as in the church; many of our leading men were in prison, suffering the penalty for having violated the law prohibit[ing] the selling of spirits to slaves." O'Connell had to deal with problems: many were supporters of the trusteeship agitation, which sought to establish ownership by the congregation rather than the diocese. He had a low opinion of their efforts: "Factions consisting of the very scum of the people were organized by some travelling merchant or barkeeper, in order to defeat the priest."[33]

During court week and other public days there was much riot and revelry. One observer declared that he often saw the streets "in a perfect riot of drunken sandhillers." Rosser Taylor comments, "The 'fighting Irish,' a small but vocal element in Columbia, doubtless accentuated the 'tumult and shouting' customarily in evidence on public days." A Hibernian Benevolent Society was formed in 1851, and some of the objects of its benevolence took up residence near the intersection of Greene and Gadson Streets, which was given the name of "New Dublin."[34]

When O'Connell became pastor of St. Peter's in 1848, he was the only priest for the mission that covered the western half of the state. He was long preceded in the area by Irish peddlers who "transversed it persistently…Their mode of disposing of their wares is of questionable morality, and can be reconciled in many cases to the principle of justice only by the fact that everybody is convinced they will cheat if they can." Despite the fact that they loyally and liberally supported their religious affiliation, their reputation created serious difficulties for an Irish priest carrying the sacraments to widely scattered adherents: "They certainly have created a very unfavorable impression on Southern society against their native country and the Catholic Church by false pretences, untruthfulness and low cunning." In his missionary travels, O'Connell encountered near disbelief by some of the inhabitants: "In towns and communities who had witnessed no other specimens of my countrymen

I was gazed at with extreme curiosity, and candidly asked if ditchers, peddlers and railroad hands did not constitute the Irish race exclusively."[35]

As they did elsewhere, the Irish—"the heavy-duty men of American progress in those days," as D.D. Wallace observed—provided the labor to build the railroads and canals. There was a need to dig canals to transport cotton to the coast. As was the case in other parts of the South, slave owners refused to use their slaves for this demanding task. The labor force was found with the Irish, many of whom had their passages paid by promoters who contracted with canal-building companies. Stories about the Irish diggers are still recalled at Landsford Canal State Park in Chester. After this work was completed in the 1820s, the workers built several public structures in Fort Mill and Rock Hill. Many of them took the opportunity to become American citizens; one group prefaced its application for citizenship with an oath in which they "absolutely and entirely renounce and adjure all allegiance and fidelity to any foreign prince, potentate, state and sovereignty whatsoever, and particularly the King of Great Britain." In all, Irish labor built eight canals in the state.[36]

In her short history of the state, Anne Riggs Osborne relates that "these Roman Catholic laborers brought their religion with them, and for the first time, Catholic churches were built in South Carolina. Strong, hard-working and adaptable, the 'Shanty Irish' soon became 'Lace Curtain,' with influence in the politics of every town where they settled." At least a few Irishmen were brought in to work on plantations for construction work. One plantation mistress asked Bishop England if he could provide a priest for her Irish workforce.[37]

The Catholic congregation in Columbia not only established a small seminary but also, in 1851, Saint Mary's College, which provided both secondary and higher education. Faced with the rising tide of nativism known as the Know-Nothing movement, the institution met with increasing hostility from some people in the city and, on occasion, had to be defended by its faculty and students. It struggled along until it was used as a Confederate facility during the Civil War and then burned in the conflagration that was part of the Union capture of the city.[38]

A Catholic church was built on Sullivan's Island in 1846, and in the same year boat builder Daniel O'Connell and merchant Michael O'Connor were responsible for the construction of St. Peter Church in Beaufort. The movement of Irish people into the Lowcountry can be seen by the formation, in 1831, of a Catholic parish in Barnwell. St. Patrick's Church in Charleston dates to 1838, but a new brick structure was built in 1886. Over time, white marble plaques, donated by families of parishioners—almost all with Irish names—were placed on the tabernacle walls. The most notable of its altar boys was James Francis Byrnes—congressman, senator, U.S. secretary of state, etc. Changing populations meant that by the 1970s, St. Patrick's had acquired an all-black congregation. A substantial number of Afro-Americans in the city were Catholics, and this would not have occurred without Irish acquiescence and support.[39]

To those Irish of the Catholic faith, there was the matter of the wake—a time of honoring and remembering a deceased family member, friend or mere acquaintance. In what many saw as a survival of paganism transferred from Ireland, these occasions often degenerated into excessive alcohol consumption, boisterousness, singing and fighting. They were a scandal to respectable Catholics and were often denounced by their priests. Another source of embarrassment to the church and Irish people themselves was the roving presence of Irish itinerants or travelers, groups of families who had been displaced from their land in Ireland and continued their nomadic way of life after they came to this country. A remnant of this group has maintained an existence at Murphy Village outside of North Augusta.[40]

As was the custom, many Irish people acquired slaves, and some people of Catholic faith in Charleston sponsored their slaves for membership in their church. One of these was John McKeegan, an Irish immigrant, wealthy blacksmith and member of the Hibernian Society, who in 1845 sponsored one of his slaves for full Catholic status. Upon his death in 1881, all of his wealth was left to the Catholic cathedral, except for his house, which he left to a former slave.[41]

The great conflict known as the Civil War not only devastated Charleston but also the Catholic Church, with its headquarters in the city and also in Columbia. With its cathedral in Charleston already in ashes before the conflict began, almost all of its property was either damaged or destroyed. Bishop Patrick Lynch's outspoken support for the Confederacy was of no avail. As has been seen, some blacks had been affiliated with that church, but with emancipation, most of them departed to set up their own church organizations. Among southern states from 1850 to 1960, only North Carolina had a lower density of Catholics in its population.[42]

Famine Time

The tragedy of the Irish famine of the late 1840s met with a generous response in South Carolina. The Hibernian Society led the relief effort. One of its members, Major Alexander Black, implored the membership to action:

> *At a period when the cry of wailing, lamentation and woe resounds throughout the land of our forefathers, when the birth place of the fathers and founders of this benevolent institution is doomed to famine, pestilence, starvation and death, while Ireland is suffering under this national calamity, it ill befits the impulses and sympathies of the heart that we should indulge in feasting and rejoicing.*

The annual St. Patrick's Day banquet was cancelled, and a relief committee, headed by Henry Connor, raised $15,000, as well as contributions of "rice, flour, cornmeal and other articles of food." The St. Patrick's Benevolent Society, established in 1817, was also active in this effort. A third society, the Charleston Irish Mutual Benevolent Society, came into being in 1849 to meet the Irish crisis. In Columbia, the Hibernian Benevolent Society was formed in 1851 for the same purpose. The South Carolina Railroad shipped the famine relief produce without charge. According to Augustine Smythe, the members of the Hibernian Society "stood with open hands welcoming to our shores those poor and distressed emigrants who fled from starvation and ruin."[43]

General Abbott Brisbane, "an ardent and idealistic Catholic" and an officer in the Irish Volunteers of Charleston, established a settlement for Irish emigrants near Albany, Georgia. Those who did migrate found themselves in a vast and isolated wilderness and sought compensation from their church for misleading them about the prospects of the scheme. The abortive settlement, concluded Dr. O'Connell, was a "thankless undertaking."[44]

Although the great majority of famine immigrants went to northern states, there was a steady flow of Irish people into Charleston and other southern ports. One effect of this was vigorous competition between free blacks and Irishmen in various trades and service occupations.[45]

The nativist or Know-Nothing movement of the early 1850s met with a muted response in South Carolina. Only a small number of politicians attempted to capitalize on the perceived influence of foreigners and Catholics in American politics. But John Cunningham of the *Charleston Evening News* thundered that Irish support for the Democratic group controlling the city government was preventing urgently needed reforms. In the wake of the 1856 mayoral election, some nativists claimed that several hundred illegal votes by newly arrived Irishmen had been cast for the winning candidate, William Porcher Miles, and that the largely Irish police force was "Paddy Miles's Bulldogs." The rise of the American Party in the city was countered by Bishop Lynch, who used pages of the *U.S. Catholic Miscellany* to denounce the movement. Despite general southern alarm that the massive wave of immigrants was strengthening the position of the North, the dominant South Carolina Democratic Party did not take the bait of nativism, which it believed would divide white people. "Slavery is the absorbing question," declared South Carolinian W.W. Boyce in 1855. "We are upon the eve of revolution, and are occupying ourselves with foreigners and Catholics, as though we had nothing at stake ourselves." Yet Jeremiah O'Connell, for one, observed an underlying antipathy to both Catholics and Irish people in the state.[46]

In the 1850s—the decade when the nativist movement was at its peak—the state government began financing the building of a rail line through the western mountain area to provide for a direct link between Charleston and the region beyond the Appalachians. In the area around Walhalla, construction of a tunnel was begun in 1854, and this work attracted a few hundred Irish itinerant workers—always a volatile element. To meet their religious needs in the growing Tunnel Hill community, the Catholic diocese constructed a small church (not surprisingly called St. Patrick's), a priest's house and a school. Hoping to restrain the construction workers' craving for alcohol, it also sponsored the St. Patrick's Temperance Society. As happened in many places throughout the country, friction between the newcomers and the older population ended in violence. In 1858, a mob that attacked the church was met by a vigorous response, as a result of which the mob leader was killed. In short order, three of the Irish defenders of the church were put on trial, convicted of first-degree murder and sentenced to death. After a lengthy agitation, led by Dr. Corcoran, editor of the *Catholic Miscellany*, their sentences were drastically reduced, and they served only a few weeks in jail. When the state legislature the next year decided to end financing of the tunnel project, almost all of the Irishmen and their families left the area. During the Civil War, the church was used as a recruiting depot, and the floor was ripped up to provide firewood.

There were other anti-Irish episodes in the period. When an Irishman was publicly whipped for talking to a slave about emancipation, bitterness became imbedded among his countrymen. "It was credibly reported," recalled Jeremiah O'Connell, "that the aggrieved individual and many of his comrades joined Sherman's army, and returned to avenge this indignity." After Columbia was occupied, they "shouted aloud with a voice that sounded through the forsaken hills, 'Hurrah for the Yankees! This is the city in which white men were whipped for talking to a negro.'"[47]

In almost all cases, however, Irish people rejected the suggestion of Frederick Douglass that Irish and Afro-Americans, facing the same basic problems, should be allies. A frequent criticism of the abolitionist movement made by Irish people in the North was that the crusaders for black emancipation ignored the exploitation of children, women and men (read Irish) in their own communities. The general attitude of Irish people in the slums of the great northern cities was that they should address the problems of discrimination, occupation and survival they faced every day, while the question of slavery way down South had nothing to do with them. Moreover, Irish people, both North and South, were often in competition with free blacks in a wide variety of occupations. There was advantage in being included in the ranks of white people.[48]

Having traveled through the eastern part of the United States immediately after the Civil War, Irish politician and newspaper proprietor John F. Maguire commented that he did not find a single Irish person in the South who supported the perpetuation of slavery, although many of them advocated a form of gradual emancipation. Of course, they were talking about slavery after it was ended, through no effort on their part—quite the contrary. Earlier, as has been seen, John England had defended slavery from its denunciation by Daniel O'Connell yet later concluded that slavery should end. However, he did not see how this could be done and left the matter in the hands of legislators. The official position of the Catholic Church was that "domestic slavery" was not immoral, stressing the responsibilities of those who had authority over slaves. Bishop Patrick Lynch of Charleston was not alone among Catholic prelates to defend the institution. During the War Between the States, Catholic clergy in the South gave vigorous support to the Confederacy, while Northern Catholic priests generally voiced commitment to the Union. In no way could it be said that Irish laymen were outspoken in rejecting black bondage. On the contrary, the evidence is complete that they fully utilized the opportunity to exploit this labor force. If most Irish-born people had few or no slaves, it was largely due to their late arrival and low economic position.[49]

According to the 1860 census, the Irish population in the state was concentrated in Charleston. Among the forty thousand white residents of the city, about 15 percent were foreign born, with more than half of these being Irish (Germans were a close second). The influx of immigrants, particularly the Irish, gave the city a white majority beginning in the late 1840s.[50]

4
Confederate Irish

In the fateful presidential election of 1860, Irish voters in the South, rather than support the candidacy of John C. Breckinridge, the choice of many other Southerners, remained loyal to the national Democratic Party and its nominee, Stephen A. Douglas. They generally viewed the national Democratic Party as their friend and protector in all parts of the country. With secession and the outbreak of civil war, however, the Irish in South Carolina, as in the rest of the region, rallied en masse to the cause of the Confederacy. The Irish Volunteer Company of Charleston is said to have been the first militia unit to volunteer for the Confederate army. The Sisters of Mercy of Charleston presented the company with a flag they had made—colored green and white, with one side having eleven stars of the Confederate states and the other side a Harp of Erin. In presenting the flag to the company, now in Virginia, Captain Edward McCrady, commanding, declared, "Sergeant McDermott: Into your hands I commit it for safe keeping. The flag will find its Jasper and its Leonard again and again among the brave men who now rally under it, as occasion demands." The heroic action of one of its members, Dominic Spellman, who carried the color standard to the end of the Battle of Gains Hill, is commemorated by a memorial tablet in the statehouse. McCrady became the most accomplished historian of the Palmetto State.[1]

Another Irish unit in the city, the Meagher Guards, quickly changed its name to the Emerald Light Infantry after Thomas Francis Meagher, a leader in the 1848 rebellion in Ireland, shifted his position from initial support for the South and decided to defend the Union. Its commander, Captain

Edward H. Ryan, was killed in the war. The Hibernian Society, whose guest speaker, Meagher, had been at its St. Patrick's Day event in 1853, proceeded to revoke his honorary membership in the organization. Among those Southern Irishmen who took strong exception to Meagher's position was Thomas McMahon of Charleston, who demanded to know how Meagher could support the cause of Irish separation from Britain and yet reject the popularly supported cause of Southern nationhood. A native of Ballingarry, County Limerick, Patrick Walsh (1840–1899) became a lieutenant in the Volunteers in 1861 but the next year moved to Augusta, Georgia, where he rose to be editor of the *Augusta Chronicle*, a state legislator, briefly a U.S. senator and, finally, mayor of Augusta.[2]

In Columbia, the Ursuline sisters presented a flag to another Irish company, the Emmett Guards of Columbia. Bishop Patrick Lynch delivered it to the unit at its encampment on Sullivan's Island. During the course of the war, this women's religious organization gained widespread respect for its care of wounded soldiers.[3]

The statistical analysis of David Gleeson has revealed that about 70 percent of Irish young men in the South served in the Confederate forces, which at least equaled the average for native-born Southerners. Given the lively involvement of young Irishmen in South Carolina in the affairs of the state, surely they at least equaled or exceeded this percentage. The involvement of the South Carolina Irish in the Confederate cause was noted by an article in the *Irish Times* in 1862 that declared that there was an "Irish Brigade" in Charleston, and "some of its officers have been publicly complimented and rewarded for their bravery." Historian Dee Dee Joyce sees the enthusiasm of the Charleston Irish for the cause as a means of solidifying their standing in the community.[4]

Bishop Patrick Lynch (1817–1882), a native of Clones, County Monaghan, arrived with several bothers, all of whom, through the building trade, acquired property and land, and all (including the bishop) became slave owners. As was the case of all other Catholic bishops in the South, Lynch was an outspoken supporter of the Confederacy; conversely, all of the Northern bishops supported the Union. Lynch conducted a battle of words with his Northern colleagues throughout the conflict, but he did more than that. In the last year of the Civil War, Lynch became an official Confederate representative in Europe. His mission obviously was to negate the Unionist activities there of Bishop John Fitzpatrick of Boston and Bishop John Hughes of New York. He was on a ship out of Wilmington, North Carolina, in April

1864 that made its last successful run through the Union blockade. While in Rome, he wrote a lengthy pamphlet defending slavery, published in several languages but not English. For his services, he was paid $1,000 (Confederate) a month. He remained in Europe until granted a presidential pardon at the end of 1865. Ex–slave owner that he was, he established a school to educate Afro-American children. He remained head of the Catholic diocese until his death in 1882.[5]

When Colonel Michael Corcoran and several other soldiers of the U.S. Sixty-ninth Regiment (later the nucleus of the Irish Brigade) were wounded and captured at the First Battle of Bull Run in July 1861, they were transported to a jail in Columbia. There they were ministered to by Dr. O'Connell, but when a jailor disrupted a Mass he was celebrating, Corcoran remarked to him, "So this is the treatment you receive at the hands of a people you seem to like so well, and serve so faithfully." Due to this disruption, O'Connell refused to conduct another service in the jail, which he claimed was the first building burned by the Union army when it seized the city in 1865. The Irish group was later transferred to Castle Pinckney in Charleston Harbor. On their way to the island, they were bombarded by rocks and curses by Irish supporters of the Confederacy. Although the official reason for holding Corcoran as a prisoner for over a year was that he was being held as a hostage to ensure that captured Confederate sailors would not be charged and punished as pirates, there was a rumor that he was being retained to prevent him, upon release, from rallying Irishmen, in both the North and South, to the cause of the Union.[6]

The Confederate cause found a powerful advocate in John Mitchel, a leading Irish nationalist who, after a long prison sentence in Australia, became a journalist and newspaper proprietor in New York, Knoxville and Richmond. One of his sons, Willie, was killed in Pickett's Charge at Gettysburg. Another son, Captain John Mitchel Jr., while in command of the artillery on Fort Sumter in the summer of 1864, after being mortally wounded reportedly declared, "I die willingly for the South, but oh! Had it been for Ireland!" He was buried in the Irish Volunteers plot in St. Lawrence's Cemetery in Charleston. In 1869, the Hibernian Society voted to erect a memorial to him.[7]

William Gilmore Simms, the son of an Irish immigrant, produced in 1863 a sixteen-part serial novel, *Paddy McGann*, which portrayed another son of Irish immigrants, complete with brogue and wit, who was able, accomplished and admirable (a forerunner to Margaret Mitchell's Patrick O'Hara, perhaps). *Paddy McGann* is seen as an allegory about the South (and

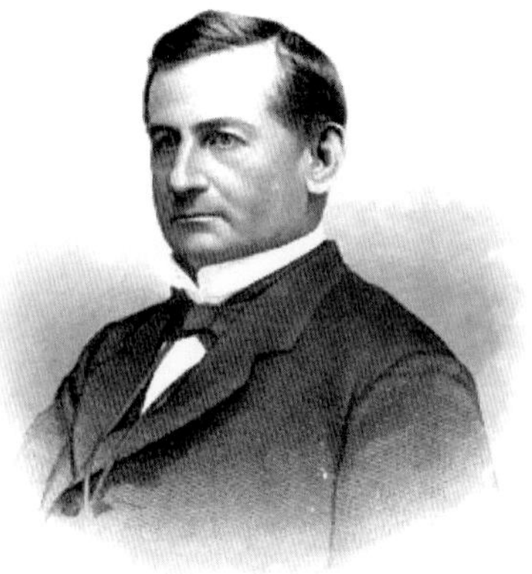

Andrew Magrath. *Courtesy of the South Carolina Library, University of South Carolina.*

the Confederacy) needing to forge an authentic literature and culture that recognized the importance of the Celtic influence in the region. Andrew G. Magrath, a past president of the Hibernian Society whose father was a 1798 refugee, had the distinction of being the last governor before General Sherman's army roared into the state at the beginning of 1865.[8]

During the course of the war, Charleston became the principal port of entry for vital supplies brought in through the Union navy blockade. It also figured largely in exports, principally of cotton, but a greater portion of cotton exports was transshipped through Mexico. John Knox, a man with a quintessential Presbyterian name, had immigrated to Charleston from Armagh in 1850. He made a fortune through the activities of his Palmetto Exporting and Importing Company and the Atlantic Steam Packet Company of the Confederate States. The fate of his fortune in the aftermath of Confederate defeat is unknown, but it probably was not entirely in Confederate currency and bonds, as he had extensive business dealings with the British colony of Bermuda.[9]

In the darkening days of the Confederacy, a controversy erupted in Columbia that could only be viewed as a mindless diversion from the threat of the catastrophe that loomed ahead. In November 1864, Dr. O'Connell, pastor of St. Peter's Church, was approached by a young couple who requested that he marry them immediately without banns being published due to the fact that they were leaving the city the next day. Although he recognized the irregularity of the situation, he proceeded to marry them. This act set off a storm of controversy in which O'Connell was charged with luring the couple into a Catholic marriage. In response to a threat, his residence was guarded by a group of Irishmen. A plan was drawn up in which, in the case that church property was torched, fires would follow throughout the city. At length, Bishop Lynch investigated the matter and exonerated O'Connell of any misconduct. As far as O'Connell was concerned, this caper was part of a pattern: "For a long time a deep-rooted feeling of opposition had been at work against the increase in Catholicity and its institutions, and at last obtained expression in this way."[10]

About the same time, there was a similar episode in Columbia. When an executed man had been given a Catholic burial presided over by a Father McNeal, a rumor spread that the priest had revived the man and that the burial had been a hoax. The controversy reached to the level of the governor, who ordered that the body be exhumed.[11]

Soon thereafter, the real threat to the city materialized with the arrival of William Tecumseh Sherman's Union army on February 17, 1865. Controversy about who burned a major part of Columbia still simmers (if not rages). With bales of cotton and barrels of whiskey lining some streets, high winds blowing, jail inmates running loose, African Americans celebrating their release from slavery, Confederate soldiers burning stores and supplies as they withdrew and then, of course, a mass of Union soldiers bursting into the capital of the heart of the rebellion, how could there not be a conflagration?

Through the night of February 17, Union soldiers rampaged through both the Ursuline Academy and St. Mary's College. In the latter, O'Connell records:

> *The rabble scrambled and scuffled to grab whatever objects came next to hand or escaped being trodden under foot. The priest who begged for the oil stocks was cursed and insulted. They drank whiskey from the chalices, passed them around as drinking cups and exalted in sacrilege. Every article of value was borne off and deposited in the booty wagons for future partition.*

Having just returned from duty as a chaplain in Confederate forces in Virginia, Father Lawrence O'Connell was dragged out and kept as a prisoner overnight. Richard Madden has recorded the assertion that Union regiments with many Catholic (read Irish) soldiers had not been sent into the city.

After Sherman's army left Columbia, there was a nasty aftermath: "A motley crowd crept from their hiding places, like the rabble at Moscow, and digging up the ruins of the College, sedulously examined every particle of the debris until scarcely a pinch of the ashes remained." O'Connell was surprised that apparently respectable people joined in the scavenging, and "when warned to desist, they reluctantly withdrew, only to return in a fresh gang by stealth, or under the cover of night." Attempts to secure compensation for destruction of the property by Union soldiers met with the response that the fire that had destroyed the facility was started by Confederate troops while burning cotton bales. Eyewitness accounts that no fires were burning before Union soldiers came into the city were of no avail.[12]

In Charleston, the position of the Catholic Church was equally dire. The Cathedral of St. Finbarr had burned down in 1860. St. Joseph's Church had been hit by two shells. On Sullivan's Island, although Confederate forces had occupied every other church and house there, the Catholic church had been left alone. When Union forces took over, they threatened to use the building as a theater, but the commanding general vetoed the idea.[13]

5
Times of Trouble and the Twentieth Century

In the aftermath of defeat and destruction, South Carolina entered a period of racial upheaval and political controversy. The Hibernian Society, struggling to survive, ceased to provide assistance to needy Irish immigrants, very few of whom arrived in this period. Due to massive disruption, the Catholic Church lost ground in the state. To raise funds, in 1868 Bishop Lynch gave lectures in which he claimed that Phoenicians had explored North America long before Columbus. (It is a wonder that he did not make this claim for St. Brendan the Navigator, the Irish missionary who penetrated the far reaches of the Atlantic in the fifth century.) The situation had improved enough by 1869 for the *Southern Celt* newspaper to begin publication in Charleston; the paper apparently continued until the early 1870s.[1]

Patrick Lynch, for one, saw excellent opportunities for Irish immigrants at this time. In a long letter in 1867 to John F. Maguire, an Irish member of parliament and publisher, the bishop of Charleston extolled the virtues of the Palmetto State. Referring to the largely Protestant immigration to the state in the eighteenth century, Lynch declared, "This Irish immigration almost took possession of the State. Irish family names abound in every rank and condition of life...South Carolina is, probably, the most Irish of any of the States of the Union." A warm welcome could be expected:

> *While its inhabitants have always had the impetuous character of the Irish race, nowhere has there been a more earnest sympathy for the struggles of Irishmen at home; nowhere will the Irish immigrant be received with a greater welcome, or be more generously supported in all his rights.*

Economic opportunity beckoned: "I do not know any part of the country where *industry and sobriety* would ensure to the immigrant who engages in agriculture an ample competence for himself and family within a briefer number of years." In regard to the black majority in the state, Lynch opined, "Now that negro slavery has been abolished, the negroes are gradually retiring to the seacoast."

Maguire urged Irish people to move out of the urban congestion of the northern states. An Irishman, he declared, "living from hand to mouth in one of the great cities as a day-labourer [could] improve his condition by betaking himself to his natural and legitimate avocation—the cultivation of the soil." The division of plantation lands in the South offered this opportunity. Maguire cited an example of a man from County Kildare twenty-three years before who had developed a prosperous farm a few miles outside Charleston. But Lynch's hopes were dashed and Maguire's advice ignored. There was no appreciable Irish migration into South Carolina or any other part of the South in the post–Civil War period or since. Despite efforts made to encourage European immigration, in 1860 there were twenty-three hundred fewer foreign-born people in South Carolina than there had been twenty years before.[2]

The movement for Irish self-government found support in Charleston with the formation of a local branch of the revolutionary Fenian Brotherhood immediately after the conflict ended. Hibernicus, in July 1865, declared, "Our city, just recovering from fire and civil war in its worst shape, cannot be expected to do much for the noble cause at present. But the return of peace, civil law and commerce will speedily restore the broken power of the Irish element." Its longtime "centre" was Captain James Power, a native of County Kilkenny who fled from Ireland in the wake of the 1848 rebellion, served in the Charleston Irish Volunteers and established a boat-building business in the city. In 1869, the Hibernian Society of Charleston donated forty dollars to the Irish revolutionary organization led by Jeremiah O'Donovan Rossa. The same year, there was contention among the society's members concerning allowing the use of its hall for a speaking engagement for John O'Neill, the Fenian "general" who led the abortive attack on Canada the next year. That concluded the society's involvement with Irish revolutionary nationalism.[3]

One of the bright spots for the state's Irish community in this period was the emergence of Michael Patrick O'Connor. Son of an emigrant from Charville, County Cork, O'Connor was a political moderate, prolific orator and noted lawyer. President of the Hibernian Society, founder of the Catholic parish in Beaufort and member of the state legislature, he was elected to Congress as a Democrat in 1878. He conducted a national speaking tour in support of the Irish land agitation following in the wake of the address to the House of Representatives by Charles Stewart Parnell. A promising political career was cut short by his death in 1881. A Charleston group supported both the Irish land agitation and the campaign for Irish home rule in the 1880s.[4]

During the period of Reconstruction, there were very few people of Irish identity in the state or region who supported the entry of African Americans into participation in government. Remaining faithful to the Democratic Party, Irishmen, North and South, rejected the overtures of the Republicans. Many Irish people had been in competition with blacks in a variety of occupations before emancipation; now that slavery had ended, the Negroes were greatly enhanced rivals. The Fenian group in Charleston viewed the Fifteenth Amendment (protecting black voting rights) "as a despotic infraction of the rights of the southern people." Irish opposition to Reconstruction won them new respect and acceptance by the white political class.[5]

Yet there remained strong opposition to Catholicism and those of that faith in the upcountry part of the state. The construction of a Catholic church in Greenville in the late 1870s generated heated denunciation from Protestant pulpits and threats of violence. The storm, however, soon abated, and the Catholic parish remained and grew.[6]

Twentieth Century

During the Progressive era, Richard I. Manning served as governor from 1911 to 1915. The great-grandson of an immigrant from Granard, County Longford, Ireland, Manning supported expanded educational opportunities, electoral reform and welfare legislation.[7]

During this period, the Irish urban political style found representation in John P. Grace, who served as reform mayor of Charleston from 1911 to 1915 and from 1919 to 1923. No detail was overlooked when Grace presided at the official welcome provided to Eamon DeValera when the president of the rebel Irish Republic visited the city in April 1920. Grace became a leading advocate for Irish self-government, serving as an officer in the Friends of Irish Freedom organization. This event was followed by other Charleston meetings supporting that cause. Grace's spirit of civic enterprise has been renewed by Joseph Patrick Riley, who has served as mayor for thirty-five years, first elected in 1975.[8]

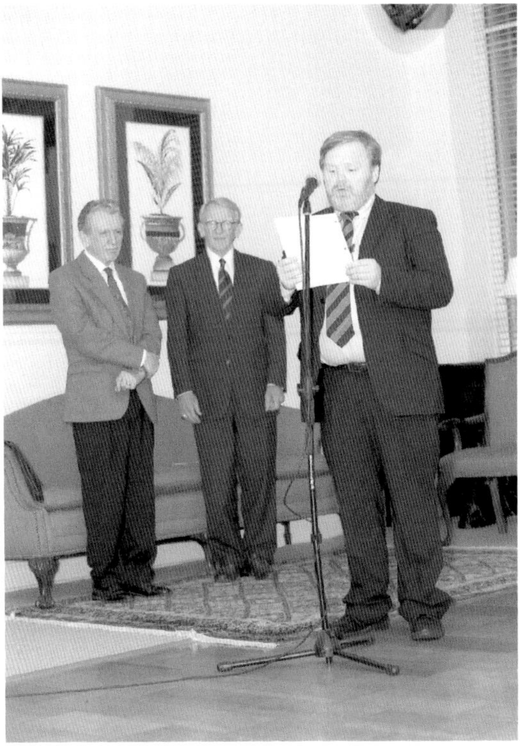

Mayor Joseph P. Riley, with Arthur Mitchell and David Gleeson. *Courtesy of Penny Hoey Photography.*

Outside Charleston, there has not been an overtly Irish presence in politics. Born to Irish parents in Charleston, James Francis Byrnes, former altar boy at St. Patrick's Church, served as a congressman, senator, governor and secretary of state under Harry Truman but established his political base in the midlands.

Two recent political figures of Irish origins are former governor Richard Riley and secretary of education in the Clinton administration and former attorney general Charles Condon of Charleston. A source of satisfaction for many people of Irish identity in the state was the narrow (and, to some, surprising) plurality in South Carolina of John Fitzgerald Kennedy in the 1960 presidential election. Ted Riley of Greenville, chairman of the Democratic State Committee and an upholder of all things Irish, had the pleasure, amidst great cheering, of telephoning Bobby Kennedy with the good news. His son Richard, after serving two terms as governor, as secretary of education was part of President Bill Clinton's involvement in Northern Ireland, which culminated in the multiparty agreement to share political power and a general peace in embattled Ulster. Making his first visit to the "Old Country" at the age of ninety, Ted traveled with his son to County Cavan, the ancestral base of the Rileys/O'Reillys, and had the life of Riley in his time there.[9]

The Ancient Order of Hibernians (AOH), which dates to 1836, has expanded to divisions in Charleston, Columbia, Fort Mill, Myrtle Beach, Greenville, Hilton Head and Beaufort. As a prelude to St. Patrick's Day in March 2004, the midland's branch presented a ceili at the state museum, which sponsors an annual ethnic heritage program at which there is appropriate

Irish (and Scottish) representation. From a purely Irish perspective, the AOH membership is limited to Catholics. Despite a plethora of local groups, there is no national organization celebrating Irish heritage in this country. In 2004, the governor designated March as Irish-American Heritage Month. There are courses in Irish history and literature at the University of South Carolina and the College of Charleston. Dr. Jack Weaver was instrumental in organizing two Scotch-Irish heritage festivals at Winthrop University in Rock Hill in 1980 and 1983. The papers presented at the conferences provide important insights into the involvement of Irish people in the history of the Palmetto State. Southern regional meetings of the American Conference for Irish Studies were held at the College of Charleston in 1995 and the University of South Carolina in 1998. Organized by Dr. David Gleeson, a conference on "The Irish in the Atlantic World" was held at the College of Charleston in March 2007.[10]

The South Carolina Irish Historical Society, under the leadership of Judge Michael Patrick Duffy and Tommy Condon, noted restaurateur, was established in 1985 as a social organization of Charleston business and professional people that sponsors an annual lecture on their favorite ethnic topic. In conjunction with the Hibernian Society and the Charleston division of the Ancient Order of Hibernians, the society is working toward the creation of a South Carolina Irish Memorial on land donated by the City of Charleston.[11]

Under the direction of Jim Lawracy, the Saint Columba Division of the Ancient Order of Hibernians in Columbia erected a memorial of granite blocks recovered from the demolished Central Correctional Institute commemorating the Irishmen who dug the Columbia Canal. Dedicated on September 6, 2008, the memorial stands in the Riverfront Park.[12]

In observing its Irish heritage, South Carolina had been a long way behind Georgia. Savannah has an Irish festival in February, followed by the extravagant St. Patrick's Day parade in March. Georgia Southern University has an Irish studies center. But Charleston's St. Patrick's Day observances have grown considerably beyond the promenade of Hibernian Society members. Beginning in 1982, a semi-Irish St. Patrick's Day festa (with rock bands galore, but in 2004, with only one Celtic musical group) has been held in Columbia. Since 1984, an Irish Children's Summer Program, initiated by Mary Ellen O'Leary, has brought about one hundred young people annually from both communities in Belfast to Columbia, Greenville, Spartanburg, Anderson and Laurens County. As has happened in most American cities, Irish-style pubs have appeared (or have been resurrected) in Charleston, Columbia, Greenville, Beaufort and Myrtle Beach. Some of these places even serve food! Being Irish, it is assumed that they are lively, fun-filled establishments with no Presbyterian (back-door) entrances.

The historical side has also gained attention. David Heisser of the Citadel, the biographer of Patrick Lynch, and David Gleeson of the College of Charleston, author of *The Irish in the South, 1815–1877*, are in the process of producing a guide to Irish landmarks in the Charleston area. Stephan White is leading a group to establish an Irish historical center. Among those Carolinians who have a continuing interest in the Irish story in the state are Donald Williams of the Hibernian Society of Charleston, who produced *Shamrocks and Pluff Mud*, and Sam Thomas of the York County Museum, author of *The Dye Is Cast: The Scots-Irish and Revolution in the Carolina Back Country*. Denis Bergin has been most active in spelling out James Hoban's time in Charleston.

Beginning in 2008, activity in Charleston around St. Patrick's Day was greatly expanded with the launching of the Irish Cultural Festival in the week leading up to the great day. The activities include lectures, concerts, readings and Irish film screenings. Denis Bergin was the able coordinator and general impresario of the 2010 event.[13]

There is certainly no lack of St. Patrick's Day activity around the Palmetto State. There are parades in Charleston, Columbia, Hilton Head and Myrtle Beach. In an effort to make Columbia's celebration less of a general street event and more focused on the significance of the day, an Irish Authentication Committee has been established. In Spartanburg, Shamrock's in the Square is a celebration held in Morgan Square in the city center, while in Greenville five Irish pubs and restaurants observe the day. In Columbia, the city's division of the Ancient Order of Hibernians presents a ceili of dance and music. St. Patrick's Day in the Charleston area at Mount Pleasant is celebrated in a unique way with "Catch the Leprechaun," a five-kilometer run followed by food, beverages and music at the Mount Pleasant Waterfront Park.

There are a variety of place names of Irish origin around the state. They include the communities of Aiken, Belfast, Bradley, Cayce, Conway, Dillon, Gaffney, Hanahan, Jackson, Londonderry, Lynchburg, Manning, Newry and Snoddy. Some places, such as Irishtown, have faded into history.

According to the 1990 census, in South Carolina people of Irish extraction represent 14 percent of the population, with German being 15 percent and English 12 percent. As is the case across the nation, South Carolina has succeeded in putting behind the blight of racism while becoming increasingly aware of the healthy and stimulating factor of ethnic diversity. As would seem appropriate, Irish-Americans are in the forefront of this development. *Erin go bragh!*[14]

Appendix
The Irish in North Carolina

In an 1899 anthology, North Carolina was described as the "Ireland of America," with this description not meant to be complimentary.

In any study of South Carolina, the natural question to arise is: what about North Carolina? My long-term research has been on the Irish in the Palmetto State, where I live, but I think that some cursory, and inadequate, attention should be given to the Green and Orange Irish in the Tar Heel State. Mary Patricia McPhail, among others, would appreciate this.

The two groups from Ireland that immigrated to the thirteen colonies played major and minor roles in the early history of North Carolina. The Scotch-Irish, with a plethora of grievances against English control in Ireland and the colonies, were by far the largest group, while many of the small group of people of original Irish stock joined in the upheaval. As was the case throughout the Appalachian region, those of Irish and Scottish origins were a formative—indeed, dominant—force in shaping the culture and customs of western North Carolina.

The present site of North Carolina was in the part of the New World that was first explored and, in time, settled by people from the British Isles. As such, it was the earliest place in America to which the Irish came. Walter Raleigh became involved with affairs in Ireland in the 1580s, when the English government gave him a grant of forty thousand acres in Cork and Kerry. He also received another grant—for a large area of the southeastern coast of what later became the United States. Raleigh planned and financed three expeditions to Roanoke Island on the Atlantic coast.

The First Irish in America

In 1585, to direct the first colony, Raleigh selected Ralph Lane, the sheriff of County Kerry in Ireland, to be governor. Serving under Lane's military leadership were John White, a skilled artist, and Thomas Harriot, an experienced scientist. They explored and described large areas of American territory and collaborated in gathering information, making maps and painting very clear and detailed watercolor pictures of the native people and their houses and boats, as well as wildlife.

Failing to receive timely supplies from home, after eleven months Lane returned to Britain with his colony in 1586. In 1589, he was named muster-master general and clerk of the check in Ireland. He was badly wounded in an Irish rebellion in 1594 but continued to serve in Ireland until his death in 1603. Among the men who remained nearly a year with Lane's colony, there were several other Irishmen: Darby Glande (Glaney or Glavin, as it also appears in the records) and Edward Nugen or Nugent, identified as Lane's servant and who had probably been in Kerry earlier with Lane. Others among this first British colony in America, who obviously were Irish, were John Costigan and Edward Kelly.

In 1587, as the final phase of his plan to colonize America, Raleigh chose John White to be governor. Among the 117 colonists, this time there were 17 women and 9 boys, including at least 1 nursing baby. Clearly intending to lay the foundation of a permanent settlement, Raleigh enlisted people with varied abilities, occupations and nationalities. Among White's colonists was Glande, crossing the Atlantic a second time, and Elizabeth Glane, who probably was his wife. Elizabeth, however, arrived at Roanoke Island alone as Darby deserted in Puerto Rico. Yet Elizabeth may not have lacked for companionship in the New World, as Irishmen Denice Carrell, Thomas Butler and James Lasie were also aboard.

Although this was a short-lived colony, it is distinguished in American history because Governor White's nineteen-year-old daughter, Eleanor, wife of colonist Ananias Dare, was among the settlers. On August 18, 1587, she gave birth to Virginia, the first British child born in America. Just as in the case of the Lane colony, supplies did not arrive when expected, and Governor White returned home to try to expedite their shipment. Difficulties at home delayed his return to Roanoke Island, the colonists disappeared and later efforts to locate them were fruitless. White retired to one of Raleigh's estates in the south of Ireland and spent the remainder of his life at Newtown in the

Great Wood of Kilmore in County Cork. As late as 1593, he was still hoping that members of the lost colony might be found.

In 1866, the British Museum acquired a portfolio of John White's watercolor drawings in Ireland. In the late twentieth century, the ruins of the house believed to have been occupied by White were discovered. The historian David B. Quinn, a native of Ireland, while compiling his book *The Roanoke Colonies* in the 1950s, examined documents, trying to learn the origin of John White, but was unable to determine whether he was Irish or English.

In 1607, a new colony began at Jamestown; this year also marked the beginning of the flow of lowland Scots into eastern Ulster. The first permanent settlers reached the Carolina region about 1650. With the restoration of the monarchy following the Civil War, there was renewed interest in the vast region. In 1663, King Charles II granted to eight of his supporters a broad belt of land south of Virginia that extended from the Atlantic Ocean to the Pacific.

It also was royal policy to encourage Scottish migration to Ireland, and it took little imagination to make America a destination. The Scots newly settled in Ulster succeeded too well. In time, they contributed to overpopulation and proved to be serious competitors with the English in the production of linen and woolen cloth. Following the defeat of the Scots at the Battle of Culloden Moor in 1746, even Scottish-held land was assigned to victorious English army officers, and the struggle to get to America became frantic.

An Irish Naturalist

One of the earliest Carolinians to be clearly identified as Irish was Dr. John Brickell, a physician who was practicing in Edenton, North Carolina, in 1729. He is best recognized today as the compiler of the natural history of North Carolina, gleaned from the writings of his contemporaries, fellow naturalists John Lawson and John Clayton. This work, printed in Dublin in 1737, was based on folk practices and remedies. Among the subscribers were medical men, apothecaries and surgeons. Many Irish family names long found in North Carolina are represented among those who subscribed to Brickell's book: Connor, Carson, Delany, Dobbin, Durham, Fergus, Gordon, Hill, Mitchell, Pierson and Richardson. Their early association with this work suggests that it may have drawn their attention to the colony. Brickell made many comparisons between his native land and North Carolina, observing that in the colony,

> *all manner of Game is here very plenty, neither are there any Laws here to bind their Priviledges,* [sic] *as it is with us in Ireland, for the meanest Planter may, with as much Freedom, destroy all manner of Game, as he that is the most Wealthy, or highest in Dignity.*

After people of Scottish descent appeared in large numbers in Ulster, the descriptive term Scotch-Irish (or Scots-Irish) eventually came into use. More often than not, the Irish were of the Roman Catholic faith, while the Scots were Presbyterians. As was the case throughout Ireland (and elsewhere) religious affiliation generally was not strongly imprinted. This was even more the case in the wilds of the American colonies, where there was a general lack of church organization and clergy of the established denominations. In the course of events in Ulster, people of these backgrounds intermarried until today only rarely are there families entirely of one or the other. Occasionally, someone was described in the records as "meer" Irish, which had a derogatory connotation. The more recent term "lace-curtain Irish" was not heard in North Carolina because none are known to have created neighborhoods, occupational bonds or religious fraternities to which the term was applied. If any chose to come or were sent to the state during the potato famine in Ireland, they were few in number and melded into existing communities. Nevertheless, before 1835, much of North Carolina was economically depressed and was sometimes referred to as "the Ireland of America."

The Irish usually were as proud of their ancestry as if they had been members of ancient noble families. Books bearing armorial bookplates of Irish families from eighteenth-century North Carolina families survive in the North Carolina Collection at the University Library in Chapel Hill. *The Colonial Records of North Carolina* contains a letter from December 2, 1769, from Edanus (Aedanus) Burke to his kinsman Dr. Thomas Burke in North Carolina, expressing full appreciation of their common family heritage. Referring to themselves as "Native Irish," the writer declared that his reading of Geoffrey Keating's history of Ireland had inspired him with a renewed sense of ethnic pride. The Irish, he noted, were of "the old Milesian race," descendants of people taken there by descendants of the sons of an Iberian king, Milesius, around 1300 BC. In 1782, Dr. Burke received another letter in the same spirit. Archibald Maclaine, a North Carolina legislator, apparently had been described as a Scotsman, and he was correcting that impression. He was only "half a Scotchman," as his mother was Irish. There, without question, was a Scotch-Irishman!

In North Carolina

Large tracts of land in North Carolina were granted on very generous terms to newcomers, as well as to groups of interested investors. New products began to be exported, and by 1735, it was reported that flax had been grown in the colony. A few years later, flaxseed was sent from North Carolina to Pennsylvania, where port facilities were better for shipment abroad. Several royal governors and other officials of Scotch-Irish origin encouraged settlement of the colony to increase productivity and a larger tax revenue—to the advantage of their political records. Some newcomers acquired thousands of acres of undeveloped land in their own names, while others formed land companies in hope of promoting settlement at a profit. Such activity brought in thousands of settlers from the north of Ireland.

The flow of Ulster Protestants to the colonies alarmed British authorities in Ireland, as this was seen as weakening the position of the loyalist population. Anglican Archbishop King was filled with concern: "No papists stir…The papists being already five or six to one, and being a breeding people, you may imagine in what conditions we are like to be in." The ill treatment of emigrants on board a ship from Dublin to North Carolina in 1735 provided the Irish Parliament with an opportunity to try to obstruct this trade. Most emigrants from Ireland in the eighteenth century arrived at Philadelphia and New York; as the land filled up in those areas, people began migrating southward toward the Carolinas.

In the 1730s, Henry McCulloh, a native of Ulster, took advantage of his position as surveyor, inspector and controller of revenues and land grants to secure huge areas of land and began to bring in settlers from the north of Ireland. Beginning in 1747, an Irish settlement was established in the northwestern Carolina frontier; this grew to be the largest community in the area. In 1755, the town of Salisbury was established there. It was there where young Andrew Jackson studied law. Another future president, also of Scotch-Irish stock—James K. Polk—was born in Pineville, North Carolina.

The further development of North Carolina was fostered by two other Irish-born leaders. Beginning in the late 1740s, Matthew Rowan, a native of County Antrim (after whom Rowan County was named) served, variously, as president of the colonial council, surveyor-general and acting governor. At this time, Arthur Dobbs began gathering land grants in the colony. A native of Carrickfergus, County Antrim, Dobbs served in a variety of government positions in Ulster and, in 1754, was appointed governor of North Carolina, a post he held for eleven years. During that time, he facilitated the movement of several boatloads of people from Ulster to his lands in Mecklenburg County (which contains modern Charlotte).

Dobbs, together with another Ulster-born land speculator, did a great deal to stimulate Irish immigration to North Carolina, but many of those who were lured found that they had become victims of local political elites who exploited them for all kinds of taxes. The response was the backcountry Regulator movement. John McDonnell, a native of County Antrim who became a merchant in Wilmington, North Carolina, observed the resulting conflict. He opposed the Regulators, which action came back to haunt him with the outbreak of the Revolution. Charged with breaking the Continental Congress's ban on the importation of British goods, one of his shiploads was confiscated and he was condemned for not upholding the new cause of American freedom. Prudent man that he was, he shortly left for Charleston, South Carolina, before returning to Ulster. His final move brought him to Cork.

Producing what is probably the first travelogue of the continental colonies, in 1753 the Irish-born Anglican clergyman James MacSparran had a most negative view of the sparsely settled North Carolina. He found that

> *the greater part of the People are necessarily rude and illiterate, irreligious and prophane. There are a very small Number of Presbyterians with some Quakers; and whatever these are, at least predominate, you shall never fail to find Immoralities and Disorders prevail…Upon the whole, this Province may still pass for a pretty wild and uncultivated Country; and excepting for the better Sort, its white inhabitants have degenerated into a State of Ignorance, not much superior to the native* Indians.

His book, *America Dissected*, published in Dublin, certainly did not suggest that his countrymen head for what he saw as the land of Indian corn, tar, turpentine, whalebone and oil.

REVOLUTIONARY IRISH

According to local tradition, it was the Scotch-Irish of Mecklenburg County who anticipated the action of the Continental Congress by a declaration of independence in 1775. Additionally, there is the tradition that the Scotch-Irish in North Carolina, as well as in Pennsylvania, were a major force in driving forward the independence movement. On the other hand, there were many in this group who remained uninvolved, and some were Loyalists. An important Loyalist group in the state was the Scottish Highlanders, whose members, in exchange for land grants, had taken oaths of allegiance to the Crown.

In the backcountry, where the Scotch-Irish were concentrated, the Regulator movement—designed to limit the near monopoly of power by those in the eastern part—had been defeated. As a result, at the beginning there was little, if any, enthusiasm for the revolt. Historian A. Roger Ekirch, in *Poor Carolina*, goes as far as to say, "Many former Regulators, perhaps a majority, simply decided to sit the Revolution out as best they could," while some became Loyalists. John Adams, that keen observer of events, declared that "the back part of North Carolina" provided the chief instance of people rising "in large bodies" against Whig (Patriot) leadership, this due to the Regulator episode. Ekirch concludes, "In few other colonies did revolutionaries go to war with so little popular support."

In North Carolina, as elsewhere, people from the other Irish background also were very much involved in the Revolution. Most notable of these was Thomas Burke (1747–1783). As was the case of his kinsman Aedanus Burke, Thomas was part of the Burke clan of Galway, of Norman origin, but now disposed of their land and political power through the political upheavals of the previous century. As Burke himself described his situation, he was "born in Ireland of a once affluent Family…some Family misfortunes reduced [him] to the alternative of Domestick Indolent Dependence, or an Enterprising Peregrination." He chose the latter course. Burke's family retained enough wealth for him to briefly study medicine at Trinity College, Dublin, before he departed for America, arriving in Virginia in 1759. He changed his profession from medicine to law, joining up with Aedanus. From the beginning of his time in Virginia, Burke engaged in political controversies, employing his poetics in satire, as well as praise for his new-found land: opposing the Stamp Act, he declared "Triumph America! Thy patriot Voice has made the Greatest of Mankind rejoice." In 1771, he moved to North Carolina, where at Hillsboro he eventually built up a large plantation that he called Tyaquin after his family's ancestral land in Galway. Immediately, he plunged into revolutionary politics, first as an opponent of the Stamp Act. His use of abrasive language, as well as a capacity for poetic expression, won him public notice. His public proclamation of himself as "a passionate Lover of Liberty and Hater of Tyranny" clearly spoke to the heritage of his Irish experience. He quickly rose in the ranks of the supporters of independence, serving first in the provincial assembly and then in the Continental Congress, where he was a strong supporter of states' rights in resisting attempts of the Continental Congress to assert control over state militias. He could be a powerful opponent, as seen in his indictment of the conduct of General John Sullivan at the Battle of Brandywine, "whose evil conduct was forever productive of misfortunes." He appears to have had a mercurial personality, possessing both charm and a steely determination. His biographer, John Watterson, refers to Burke's "penchant for controversy." He often employed poetic skill as a weapon against opponents, but he was also capable of deep sentiment—as when he sometimes decried his position as a "homesick pilgrim" desirous of returning to his "Native Country." Burke has been described as being of "Middle Stature, thin visage, Much Mark'd with Small Pox," as well as blind in his right eye. His satirical assaults on opponents were met in kind; one opponent expressed, in part, admiration for his ability: "Burke's eye, in double sense, is single, Enabling truth with wit to mingle."

In June 1781, in the midst of the British invasion of the new state, he achieved the dubious distinction of being elected governor at the early age of thirty-five. He saw this situation with which he was confronted

> *everywhere unprepared for defense, without arms, without discipline, without arrangements, even the habits of civil order and obedience to laws, changed into a licentious contempt for authority and a disorderly indulgence of violent propensities.*

Against the odds, he effectively rallied opposition to the looming threat of a British incursion. The British had a powerful base at the port of Wilmington, which was the rallying point of a Loyalist force led by David Fanning. A Tory raid led by Fanning captured Burke and other state officials in September, and he was imprisoned at Sullivan's Island in Charleston Harbor. Refused parole as a potential hostage should Fanning be captured by the rebels, he managed to escape in January 1782. He resumed his duties as governor but did not seek reelection in 1782. Deeply in debt, he hoped to recover his fortune through farming. Anticipating his wishes, his kinsman Aedanus Burke took steps to buy him a plantation in Georgia. Suffering from increasing illness, and shortly after the birth of his only child, he died in December 1783 at the young age of thirty-six.

James and Maurice Moore were from a branch of the noted Moore family of South Carolina. Both of them were active in the agitation for independence in North Carolina, with James rising to the rank of brigadier general and responsible for the Patriot victory at Moore's Creek Bridge in February 1776. Maurice was a jurist and legislator. Both brothers died in 1777. Maurice's grandson, also named Maurice, wrote a biography of Edward Lacey, the Revolutionary War general.

Another general in the Continental army was James Hogun (or Hogan), who was one of about fifteen Irish-born soldiers to rise to that high rank during the Revolution. He was born in Ireland about 1731 and emigrated in 1751, settling in Halifax County, North Carolina. He began his support for American independence in 1774 as a member of the Halifax Safety Committee and represented his county in several provincial congresses. His military career began when he was appointed major of the Halifax militia in April 1776, quickly rising to the rank of colonel of the Seventh North Carolina Continentals the following November. In July 1777, he joined George Washington's army in Pennsylvania, where he fought in the Battles of Brandywine and Germantown. He then returned to North Carolina to raise four new regiments for the Continental army, two of which he led north to combat at White Plains, New York. From there, he led the newly formed North Carolina Brigade to Philadelphia. When he became commander in the Philadelphia area, he was appointed a brigadier general. More action followed. Confronted with a severe winter, he led his brigade on a seven-hundred-mile trek south to the defense of Charleston, South Carolina, arriving on March 3, 1780. When the defending Patriot army was forced to surrender under British assault on May 12, he was made a prisoner of war and was placed in captivity in what is now Mount Pleasant. Refusing parole in order to stay with his men, he died in captivity in January 1781.

Another Irish-born general was Matthew Locke, who was born in the north of Ireland in 1730 and immigrated at age twenty-two to settle in Salisbury, North Carolina, which was originally called the "Irish settlement." After substantial political involvement, he became a brigadier general, not of the fighting sort, but as a paymaster. He later served as a congressman.

Thomas McGuire was an Irishman who took a different course in the Revolution. Born in Dublin around 1730, he studied law in London. By 1760, he was in North Carolina, where he served as a judge in the vice admiralty court and, beginning in 1767, as attorney general of the colony. Although he did not support the independence movement, he was offered his former position of attorney general in 1779 but declined to serve. After the Revolution, in 1785, he went to England, where he was successful in gaining compensation as a Loyalist.

Redmond Burke, brother of Governor Burke, followed the same route. He came to North Carolina from Ireland in 1769 and indifferently pursued various occupations. He served as a surgeon in the colonial militia but, he claimed, left the military when the Patriot objective became independence. His house at Cornbakee Ferry was burned by British forces, and while living in England in 1782, he sought compensation for this loss.

An important political figure in North Carolina in the early period of independence was William Joseph Gaston (1778–1844), whose father, a medical doctor, was born in Ireland during the revolution. His son became a lawyer of notable achievement but, more importantly, a congressman of strong Federalist beliefs; he fought the losing battle against the rising tide of Jacksonian democracy. One of the few prominent Catholics in the state, Gaston concluded his public career as a member of the state supreme court. Gaston County and Gastonia are named in his honor.

One indication that there was only a small number of indigenous-stock Irish people in North Carolina during the colonial period is that there were few Catholics there. James Garzia, an Anglican missionary in 1741, reported that there were an even dozen Roman Catholics in the colony. Writing from the port town of New Bern in 1769, Reverend James Reed declared, "As for papists, I cannot learn there are above nine or ten in the whole County." Five years later, Governor William Tryon reaffirmed that belief: "Every sect of religion abounds here except the Roman Catholic." The first known Catholic priest in North Carolina was Patrick Cleary, a native of Ireland who arrived at New Bern in 1784 and served there until his death in 1790. For many years, New Bern remained a small outpost in the Catholic diocese of Charleston, despite the rise in the numbers of Tar Heel Catholics. Until 1835, Catholics were barred from public office by the state constitution, which required an affirmation of the truth of Protestant teachings.

Although the great mass of people of some Irish connection (the Scotch-Irish) came into North Carolina from the overland route, people from other parts of Ireland trickled in from the coast. One of the fortunate ones was Connor Dowd, who landed in 1754, illiterate and devoid of any resource except for some Irish linen. This plucky Celt proceeded to hawk the material through the backcountry, and within twenty years he owned seven thousand acres, plus slaves, furniture and other property worth £10,000.

In the 1830s, a small number of Irish miners was brought in to work the gold deposits along the Catawba River. A Catholic priest, Timothy Cronin, making a circuit through the backcountry, sponsored a fundraising effort that resulted in the building of a small church, which was erected in 1843. With the ending of the mining venture and the establishment of the nearby Belmont Abbey, a Benedictine monastery, the building fell into disuse for a century. In 1970, however, the structure was restored, and two divisions of the Ancient Order of Hibernians in the Charlotte area gather there for Mass three times a year.

Ireland did produce an important religious figure with strong North Carolina connections. James O'Kelley (1735–1826) was living in Virginia in 1760 and then moved to Chatham County, North Carolina. In 1784, he was involved in the establishment of the Methodist Episcopal Church in this country. An opponent of the power of bishops, as well as of slavery, O'Kelley led a movement to form a separate church, which took form as the Republican Methodist Church in 1793. The next year, it was renamed the Christian Church, with authority in the hands of the congregation.

When Protestants of some sort from the north of Ireland first began to pour into the country in the colonial period, due to their reputation of being a troublesome and violent group—particularly in New England and Pennsylvania—the term "Scotch-Irish" was often used as a term of derision. Many people were glad to see the end of them, as they set off on the Great Wagon Road to the hills and mountains of the South. But with the influx of Irish and Catholic people from other parts of Ireland, beginning in the second half of the nineteenth century, it was customary for many writers to denigrate the Irish while at the same time often lauding the Scotch-Irish as wholly Scottish. Their hyphenated name, it was said, merely indicated that they had once lived in Ireland. North Carolina historians R.D.W. Connor (a very Irish name), Chalmers Davidson, Archibald Henderson and Hugh T. Lefler were among those who followed national writers Theodore Roosevelt, Frederick Jackson Turner, Thomas J. Wertenbaker and others in heaping high praise on the Scots and showing disdain for the Irish. In the late twentieth century, however, this practice was generally abandoned in favor of regarding the Scotch-Irish as one people—an amalgamation of the two.

James G. Leyburn undertook a new look at the Scotch-Irish and in 1962 published *The Scotch-Irish: A Social History*. This work demonstrates how many popularly recognized traits of the Scotch-Irish have also long been cited as qualities of the American population in general: deep religious convictions, belief in democracy and support of education. The Scotch-Irish or Ulster Scots, he pointed out, were a "people of a new nationality with its own traditions and culture and points of reference." Before the American

Revolution, colonial officials often referred to these people as Irish because they had come to America from Ireland. They were not offended by this, except when they were confused with the other kind of Irish. The cult of the Scotch-Irish from Ulster reached the point that many of these writers described Ulster as moored just west of Scotland, without any physical or cultural connection with the rest of Ireland. This whole matter, focusing on the Scotch-Irish impact in Pennsylvania, has been addressed by Patrick Griffin in his *The People of No Name*, which argued that they were just an amorphous conglomeration of people of Protestant background from Ulster. Like so many earlier writers, however, Griffin blanked out the presence of Irish people of Catholic identity, of whom there were many in Ulster, as well those from the other parts of Ireland who joined the western movement across the Atlantic. The word "Catholic" is not to be found in his index.

Professor William Powell of the University of North Carolina at Chapel Hill assessed the impact of the Scotch-Irish in the state's history. Because as individuals they are so diverse, the Scotch-Irish have not been easy for American historians to characterize as a body or to classify as individuals. R.D.W. Connor, North Carolina historian and first archivist of the United States, concluded that

> *there is perhaps no virtue in the whole catalogue of human virtues which has not been ascribed to them; no great principle of human liberty in our political and social system which has not been placed to their credit; no great event in our history which they are not said to have caused…* [T] *he Scotch-Irishman was domestic in his habits and loved his home and family; but we know also that he was an unemotional being, seldom giving expression to his affections and accordingly presenting to the world the appearance of great reserve, coldness, and austerity. He was loyal to his own kith and kin, but stern and unrelenting with his enemies. He was deeply and earnestly religious, but the very depth and earnestness of his convictions tended to make him narrow-minded and bigoted. He was law-abiding so long as the laws were to his liking, but when they ceased to be he disregarded them, quietly if possible, forcibly if necessary. Independent and self-reliant, he was somewhat opinionated and inclined to lord it over any who would submit to his aggressions. He was brave, and he loved the stir of battle… His whole history shows that he would fight, he would die, but he could never be subdued. In short, in both the admirable and his un-admirable traits, he possessed just the qualities which were needed on the Carolina frontier in the middle of the eighteenth century.*

A random examination of entries in the six-volume *Dictionary of North Carolina Biography* reveals that people bearing known Irish or apparent Irish or Scotch-Irish names predominate. In addition to those who made notable contributions to North Carolina as well as the nation, there are scoundrels, thieves, murderers and other unsavory characters. Professor Powell has investigated: of those whose biographies confirm that they are of Irish birth or descent, there will be one actor, one chart or map maker, one compiler of a stud book, two botanists, two geologists, two machinists, three merchants, three musicians, three presidents of the United States and a vice president, three state officials, four Indian traders, four writers/authors, five poets, six Confederate officers, six journalists, six planters, seven governors of North Carolina, eight federal officials, ten physicians, eleven judges, twelve military persons, twelve Revolutionary soldiers and one heroine, eighteen attorneys and eighteen clergymen.

In addition to the mere handful selected for reference here, there were hundreds more whose presence was important in the creation of the state and the nation. Dr. Powell concluded, "It has often been noted that it was the people of Scotch-Irish descent who made North Carolina the successful state that it became." This aspect of its history has been given increased focus through activity of the Ulster-American Heritage Symposium, which since 1976 has held biennial meetings alternatively in Northern Ireland and southern Appalachian universities, including the University of North Carolina at Asheville, Appalachian State University and Western Carolina University.

The other side of the Irish story has been preserved (and embellished) by the expansion of the Ancient Order of Hibernians, which has divisions in Charlotte, Salisbury, Asheville, Greensboro, Durham and Wilmington.

As in the case of South Carolina, in a questionnaire added to the 1990 census, when people in North Carolina were asked about their ethnicity, the great majority who responded that they were of Irish roots chose the category of Irish rather that Scotch-Irish. Obviously, the proponents of the primacy of the Scotch-Irish saga will need to renew their efforts. In one instance, the label "Scotch-Irish" is certainly appropriate when applied to the tradition of the distilling of fine whiskey (not to mention folk music and country and western) in the mountains of Appalachia. Time for wetting the shamrock?

An interesting side note on the Irish influence or mating with Afro-Americans is found in the career of James O'Hara, congressman from North Carolina in the 1880s. Son of an Irish seaman and a West Indian woman, O'Hara came to North Carolina from New York when Federal forces occupied parts of the coast at the beginning of the war. After being a teacher, lawyer and local government official, he was elected to Congress in 1882, serving two terms. Also in that era there was Berry O'Kelly, a successful realtor, banker and philanthropist.

The continuing interest in Irish culture is seen in several places where Irish dancing is given instruction. Additionally, the nearly ubiquitous Irish pubs have sprung up across the state, ranging from the James Joyce Pub in Durham to Hannah Flanagan's Irish Pub in Asheville. At the academic level there are courses on Irish history and literature at the University of North Carolina campuses at Chapel Hill and Wilmington, while Wake Forest has a course in Irish literature and its press has been a prolific publisher of Irish literature.

The variety of Irish activity in the Tar Heel State every March is no "small potatoes" (Scotch-Irish need apply). Without fail, on the Great Day the six divisions of the Ancient Order of Hibernians sponsors gatherings of all sorts, with the Governor Thomas Burke Division in Wake County organizing an Irish Music Festival. Raleigh has a Wearin' O' the Green Festival, complete with a parade and a Rose of Raleigh pageant. Charlotte Goes Green has a full-fledged parade, complete with green fireworks, a promenade of Irish breeds of dogs and pipe bands. Not to be outdone, in Asheville there will be a Shamrock Fun Run and a Bike of the Irish event, and most unusually, the Irish Road Bowling Association will be sponsoring a Bowl Game for the occasion. Five other places, from Hendersonville to Nags Head, will be observing the commemoration of the Patron Saint of Erin. So, in North Carolina, as elsewhere, the dreary days of late winter are brightened by splashes of green and orange.

Notes

Introduction

1. Doyle, *Ireland, Irishmen*, 75–76, 135; Pulkinen interview.
2. Edgar, *South Carolina*, 58. For this statement, Edgar provides a single reference—Edward McCrary, *South Carolina under the Royal Government*, 133–34—which describes a single episode, the difficulties faced by an Irish Presbyterian group in their settlement at Williamsburg in 1732. German settlers, a sizeable element in colonial South Carolina, are also given little attention. There are only six references to Irish, while there are ten to Germans and an amazing nine to Jews, who were less than 1 percent of the population in any period (see pp. 702, 699 and index).

   In his review of Edgar's book, Orville Burton mentions South Carolina's diversity, including "Dutch, French, Hispanics, Jews, Swedes, various other ethnic groups." The Irish are obviously included under "other." *South Carolina Historical Magazine* 100, no. 3 (July 1999): 263.

Chapter 1

1. Ramsay quoted in O'Brien, *Hidden Phase*, 356; Doyle, *Ireland, Irishmen*; Wilson, *United Irishmen*, 3–9, 52–56, 176–79.
2. Lockhart, *Aspects of Emigration*, 141.
3. *Calendar of State Papers, Colonial, 1669–74* in Silk, "Irish Abroad," 601–02.
4. Wallace, *History of South Carolina*, vol. 1, 20.

5. Melvin, "Florence O'Sullivan"; Neuffer, *Names in South Carolina*, vol. 6, no. 2; vol. 9, no. 20; Snowden and Cutler, *History of South Carolina*, vol. 1, 79; Sirmans, *Colonial South Carolina*, 31; Cantrell, *Celtic Culture*, 93–94.
6. Melvin, "John Barnwell."
7. *Warrants for Lands in South Carolina, 1672–1711*, 680–709.
8. Ibid., 37, 105, 63; Melvin, "Florence O'Sullivan," 248–49; Wood, *Black Majority*, 25.
9. *Warrants for Lands*, 507, 28–29, 172–73, 86; Ames, "Cantey Family," 203–08; Kenny, "Irish in 'the South,'" 97; MacLysaght, *Surnames of Ireland*, 36. See also McCrady, *History of South Carolina* and Padraig O'Maidan, "An Irishman's Diary," *Eire/ Ireland* (Winter 1972), 96.
10. Roper, "Unraveling"; Miller, "'Scotch-Irish,'" 139–57.
11. Miller, *Emigrants and Exiles*, 139–45.
12. *New England Historic and Genealogical Register* in O'Brien, *Hidden Phase*, 351
13. Sirmans, *Colonial South Carolina*, 200–01; Ramsay quoted in O'Brien, *Hidden Phase*, 353–55.
14. *Carolina Described More Fully*, pamphlet (Dublin, 1684).
15. Rivers, *Sketch*, 138; McCrady, *Proprietary Government*, 275; Melvin, "John Barnwell."
16. *Statutes at Large of South Carolina*, vol. 2, chapter 167.
17. *Dictionary of American Biography*, vii, 127–28; Hewatt, *Rise and Progress*, 144–45; Wallace, *Short History*, 67–68, 70.
18. Hewatt, *Rise and Progress*, 274–76; Wallace, *Short History*, 80, 101; *Biographical Directory of the South Carolina House of Representatives*, vol. 2, 468–69.
19. Lees, "Historical Development"; Smith, "Baronies of South Carolina"; Neuffer, *Names in South Carolina*; Ball, *Slaves in the Family*, 150–52.
20. Ball, *Slaves in the Family*, 34–35.
21. Melvin, "John Barnwell," l, 11; Lawson, *New Voyage*, 163.
22. Carroll, *Historical Collections*, 205; Sirmans, *Colonial South Carolina*, 123.
23. Hewatt, *Rise and Progress*, ii, 63–64; Doyle, *Ireland, Irishmen*, 63.
24. Carroll, "Irish Quaker Community."
25. Lockhart, *Emigration from Ireland*, 33; Dickson, *Ulster Emigration*, 118.
26. Wallace, *History of South Carolina*, vol. 1, 341; vol. ii, 44.
27. Woodmason, *Carolina Backcountry*, 46n., 11, 42, 60, 61, 56, 38. Woodmason believed there were "many concealed Papists" among the Presbyterians and Quakers.

28. Doyle, *Ireland, Irishmen*, 60, 72, 74, 81. Eid, "Colonial Scotch-Irish"; Eid, "Irish, Scotch"; Miller, "'Scotch- Irish,'" 11–15; O Snodaigh, *Hidden Ulster*; Cash, *Mind of the South.*
29. Doyle, *Ireland, Irishman.* A 1980 survey among adult males in the Appalachians showed that only 5 percent of them had a church affiliation. Miller, *Emigrants and Exiles*, 147.
30. Akenson, *Irish Diaspora*, 7, 224–46; Dickson, *Ulster Emigration*; Griffin, *People of No Name*, 3.
31. Chalkley, *Chronicles*, vol. 1, 440.
32. McCrady, *History of South Carolina*, 593; Hewett, *Rise and Progress*, vol. 2, 272–73.
33. *SCHGM*, v. ii (1901): 299; *Freemans Journal* [Dublin], November 1, 1780; Lockhart, *Emigration from Ireland*, 33.
34. Smith, *White Servitude*, 42.
35. *Papers of Henry Laurens*, November 9, 1768, vol. 6, 1768–1769, 150.
36. Bridenbaugh, *Cities in Revolt*, 323.
37. Smith, *White Servitude*, 42; Lockhart, *Emigration from Ireland*, 150.
38. *South Carolina Gazette*, July 20–27, 1734.
39. Bridenbaugh, *Cities in Revolt*, 333–34.
40. Miller, *Emigrants and Exiles*, 146; Crary, "Humble Immigrant."

CHAPTER 2

1. McCrady, *History of South Carolina*; Nadelhaft, *Disorders of War*, 61, 64; Miller, *Origins*, 480.
2. Biographical Directory, South Carolina House, 571–77; Taylor, *Ante-Bellum South Carolina*, 38.
3. Biographical Directory, 577–81.
4. Ibid., 419–22.
5. Coghlan, "Pierce Butler."
6. A. Burke to Dr. Burke, December 2, 1769, North Carolina Colonial and State Records, vol. 15, 676–80; Calhoon, "Aedanus Burke," 50–65; Watterson, "Thomas Burke."
7. "Diary of Timothy Ford," *SCHGM* 13 (1912): 146; Johnson, *Traditions and Reminiscences*, 428–37; *Charleston News and Courier*, September 1, 1935; Mitchell, *History of Hibernian Society*, 116–18; Meleney, *Public Life*, 272, 12,

232, 237; Doyle et al., *Irish Immigrants*, 579; Rogers, "Aedanus Burke"; Calhoon, "Aedanus Burke," 64.

8. McCrady, *History of South Carolina*, 150.
9. Ramsay, *American Revolution*; Boatner, *Encyclopedia*, 912.
10. Garden, *Anecdotes*, 279.
11. Simms, *Revolution in South Carolina.*
12. Simms, *Life of Francis Marion*, 60.
13. O'Neall, *Annals of Newberry*, quoted in O'Brien, *Hidden Phase*, 198–199; Pope, *History of Newberry County*, vol. 1, 36–37, 46, 51; Gibbes, *Documentary History*, vol. 3, 7–8.
14. Wallace, *Short History*, 264; Johnson, *Traditions*, 101n; McCrady, *History of South Carolina*, 33–34, 41–43; Snowden, *History of South Carolina*, vol. 1, 319; Miller, *Origins*, 480–81.
15. Wallace, *Short History*, 264–69; Snowden, *History of South Carolina*, vol. 1, 320.
16. Weigley, *Partisan War*, 13; O Snodaigh, *Hidden Ulster.*
17. McCrady, *History of South Carolina*, 39, 558–59, 710. See also Pope, *History of Newberry County*, 46; Wallace, *Short History*, 265. McCrady, one of fourteen children, the most prolific historian of the state in the nineteenth century, served in a key role in the 1894 constitutional convention that effectively disbarred blacks from voting. One of his brothers, John, became a noted advocate of the "science of racial differences." Edgar, *South Carolina Encyclopedia*, 607–08.
18. Snowden, *History of South Carolina*, vol. 1, 320; McCrady, *History of South Carolina*, 587.
19. Lambert, *South Carolina Loyalists*, 25–29, 306; Walsh, *Charleston's Sons*, 70.
20. Shy, "American Society," 182, n.22; Johnson, *Traditions and Reminiscences*, 101; Miller, *Origins*, 479–80. A German regiment, organized in the Continental army in 1776 and composed of soldiers from Pennsylvania and Maryland, performed disastrously, and its commander either surrendered or defected. Another German regiment, raised in Virginia, apparently performed creditably (Boatner, *Encyclopedia*, 426, 494). An effort to raise a corps of German deserters from the British army was abandoned by the Continental Congress in 1779 after recruitment failed. *Journal of Congress*, June 21, 1779, 754. A history of German settlers and the Lutheran Church in the Carolinas, after some vague statements about thousands being involved in the conflict, claims that whenever German (Hessian) mercenaries encountered German communities, they deserted from the British army. G.D. Bernheim, *History of German Settlements*, 172–

73. There were a lot of Hessian deserters: of the thirty thousand that came over, about five thousand deserted; others remained when British forces withdrew (Boatner, *Encyclopedia*, 425–26).

21. Simms, *Revolutionary War*, 86–89; Kilber, "Simms's Irish."

22. Metzger, *Catholics in the Revolution*, 173, 213; Wallace, *Short History*, 261; *South Carolina Gazette*, July 25, 1775; Walsh, *Charleston's Sons*, 71.

23. McCrady, *History of South Carolina*, 23–24; O'Connell, *Catholicity in South Carolina*, 140–41; Dabney and Dargan, *Drayton and the Revolution*, 82–83; Madden, *Catholics in South Carolina*, 14.

24. Wallace, *Short History*, 261–62.

25. Boatner, *Encyclopedia*, 730–34.

26. Chesnutt and Floyd, *Sergeant Jasper*; Wallace, *Short History*, 274. Jasper was of "obscure parentage" but was apparently from the Georgetown, South Carolina vicinity. According to another report, he was born in Georgetown. Another claim is that he was German. Blanco, *American Revolution*, vol. 1, 814. Williams, *Shamrocks*, 114, 141. Since Jasper is not an Irish name, how did the Irish connection originate?

27. O'Brien, "Pre-Revolutionary Irish," 363–68; *Journal of American Irish Historical Society* 23 (1929–30): 53.

28. Kingston-Conway/Robert Conway Marker website, www.hmdb.org/marker.asp?marker=11291.

29. O'Brien, *Hidden Phase*, 153; Wallace, *Short History*, 220, 274–75; Johnson, *Traditions of Revolution*, 99–102.

30. Walsh, "Edmund Egan."

31. O'Brien, *Irish Firsts*, 10–13.

32. *Dictionary of American Biography*, vol. 5, 48–49.

33. "Order Book of First Regiment, South Carolina Line," *SCHGM* 8 (1907): 75.

34. Following the British occupation of Charleston in May 1780, the Scottish St. Andrews Society continued to hold meetings. McCowen, *British Occupation*, 123; Elzas, *Jews of South Carolina*, 38.

35. White, *King's Mountain Men*, 139–45; Draper, *King's Mountain*, 512.

36. Collins, *Autobiography*, 12–14, 53–54.

37. Ibid., x.

38. Snoddy, "Volunteers of Ireland"; Metzger, *Catholics and Revolution*, 243–59; Landrum, *Colonial and Revolutionary History*, 338.

39. Shy, "American Society," 73–74, ref. 3, 179; Tarleton, *History of Campaigns*, 86; Doyle et al., *Irish in Land of Canaan*, 564n; Moore, *World of Toil*.

40. *Dictionary of American Biography*, vol. 526; Johnson, *Traditions of Revolution*, 461; Cullen, *Story of the Irish*, 41. A story in the Rock Hill area is that Jackson's father had a Presbyterian funeral, and by provision of his will, rum was provided for his pallbearers, which resulted in them losing the body on the way to the cemetery. Professor Jack Weaver correspondence.
41. Simms, "Francis Marion," 60, 113. According to David Ramsay, there was a substantial Irish settlement in the Williamsburg area beginning in the 1730s. Ramsay quoted in O'Brien, *Hidden Phase*, 354–55.
42. Snowden, *History of South Carolina*, vol. 1, 390.
43. Moore, *Edward Lacey*, 2–3; Lossing, *Pictorial Field Book*.
44. Guilday, *John England*, vol. 2, 367; Wallace, *Short History*, 281; Moss, *South Carolina*; Jones, *Ocean of Promise*.
45. Kennedy, *Scots-Irish*, 80–81; "History of American Women" blog, www.womenhistoryblog.com; Silcox-Garret, *Heroines of the Revolution*; Ingle, *Courageous Kate*.
46. Lambert, *South Carolina Loyalists*, 119, 275–76; Shy, *People Numerous*, 166, 187.
47. Boatner, *Encylopedia*, 312
48. Doyle et al., *Irish in Land of Canaan*, 559–67, 567n.
49. *Encyclopedia of South Carolina*, 220–21.
50. Palmer, *Biographical Sketches*, 620–21.
51. Crary, "Humble Immigrant," 59, 61.
52. Miller, "'Scotch Irish,'" 134–35.
53. *American National Biography*, vol. 16, 630–31; Editors, *Who Was Who*, 426; Meleny, *Aedanus Burke*, 108–09.
54. Kevin Whelan research on United Irishmen emigrants to the United States.
55. Miller, "'Scotch Irish'"; Kennedy, *Scots-Irish*; O'Brien, *Hidden Phase*. For O'Brien, see Doyle, *Ireland, Irishmen*, 60.
56. Fitzpatrick, *God's Frontiersmen*, 93, 166–67, 274.
57. Lambert, *South Carolina Loyalists*, 275–76.
58. Ramsay, *History of South Carolina*, vol. 1, 273–74; Wallace, *Short History*, 325; see also Mitchell, *Hibernian Society*.
59. Ahlstrom, "Captain and Chef."
60. Woods, *Dictionary of Irish Biography*, vol. 8, 630–33.

CHAPTER 3

1. Mitchell, *Hibernian Society*, 11–12; Wilson, *United Irishmen*, 43.
2. Mitchell, *Hibernian Society*, 13–18.
3. Williams, *Shamrocks*, 85–114, 245–46; Salley, "History of Volunteers," 8, 16; Mitchell, *Hibernian Society*, 51–54; WPA project, 1935–1937, copies of minutes, 1884–1901, 1915–29.
4. McCrady article, *South Carolina Historical Magazine* (1904): 62; James Armstrong centennial address, 1917; Papers of John C. Calhoun, xv, 532.
5. Freehling, *Prelude to the Civil War*, 181–82.
6. Tasistro, " Theatrical Visit," 182–83, 185–86.
7. Mitchell, *Hibernian Society*, 19; *Biographical Directory of South Carolina*, Senate, vol. 2., 1235–1236; Coghlan, "Pierce Butler"; Edgar, *Encyclopedia of South Carolina*, 12; O'Connell, *Catholicity in South Carolina*, 304–05.
8. Coit, *John C. Calhoun*; *American Portrait*, 3–4; Calhoun Papers, xv, 122, 151, 153, 431, 532, 774. Calhoun's paternal grandfather (d. 1791) was also named Patrick, and he married Catherine Montgomery (1683/4–1760), also of Donegal. O'Connell, *Catholicity in South Carolina*, 337.
9. Freehling, *Prelude to the Civil War*, 16, 181–82. See also Mills, *Statistics of South Carolina*, 176.
10. Guilday, *Bishop England*; Salley, "Irish Volunteers," 2n; Freehling, *Prelude to the Civil War*, 182, 269; Gleeson, *Irish in the South*, 109, 118–19.
11. *Dictionary of American Biography*, vol. 5, 91; Kelly, "Man Who Built the White House"; Seale, "Hoban"; information from Irvin Condon, president of the Hoban Society.
12. Killion and Moss, *Journal of Michael Gaffney*, 1–5, 28–30.
13. Mitchell, *Hibernian Society*, 15, 18.
14. O'Connell, *Catholicity in South Carolina*, 114, 220–24; Hollis, *University of South Carolina*, 78, 284; Schutte interview.
15. O'Connor, "Michael Twomey," 71–74; Wallace, *Short History*, 447, 474.
16. Carey, *Immigrant Bishop*, 87.
17. Guilday, *England*; Miller, "Roman Catholicism," 95; *Mitchell, Hibernian Society*, 45–51.
18. Miller, "Roman Catholicism," 96.
19. O'Connell, *Catholicity in South Carolina*, 239–47.
20. Doyle et al., *Irish in the Land of Canaan*, 94–102, 711.
21. *Charleston City Gazette*, December 24, 1788; Proctor, "South Carolina Ships" website.

22. Miller, "'Scotch-Irish,'" 150–53.
23. Fitzsimons Papers and biography, USC, Caroliniana Library collection.
24. Motes, *1850 Census*; Clark, "South's Irish Catholics," 201; Taylor, *Ante-Bellum South Carolina*, 38.
25. Silver, "Old South's Urbanization"; Gleeson, *Irish in the South*, 44, 100; Carl Pulkinen story.
26. Williams, *Shamrocks*, 13–14, 17–18; Porcher, *History of Santee Canal*; Morris, "White Bondage," 194–95; *Charleston Courier*, March 26, April 6, 1855.
27. Joyce, "White, Worker."
28. Carroll, *Historical Collections*; *Southern Literary Journal and Monthly Magazine* (1835–37); St. Patrick's Day address, Charleston, 1838; Speeches of B.F. Porter and B.R. Carroll, Charleston, 1848. Contents of both Carroll speeches in USC, Caroliniana Library collection.
29. Mitchell, *Hibernian Society*, 56, 60–61.
30. Miller, "Roman Catholicism," 87, 93.
31. O'Connell, *Catholicity in South Carolina*, 196–98, 209; Moore, *Columbia and Richland County*.
32. O'Connell, *Catholicity in South Carolina*, 212–13.
33. Taylor, *Ante-Bellum South Carolina*, 32; Moore, *Columbia and Richland County*, 140–41.
34. O'Connell, *Catholicity in South Carolina*, 239, 283–84.
35. Wallace, *Short History*, 374; Crowson, "Building the Lansford Canal," 17, 61; information from park ranger: Irish voices still echo!
36. Osborne, *South Carolina Story*, 71.
37. Saint Mary's College, Columbia, 1851–1865; O'Connell, *Catholicity in South Carolina*, 241–48.
38. Stella Maris Roman Catholic Church website; Rowland et al., *Beaufort County*, 381; Mitchell, *Hibernian Society*, 80. *Story of Memorial Shrine of St. Andrew the Apostle, Barnwell*, booklet (1945); Doherty, *St. Andrew's Chapel*, booklet (1978); Madden, *South Carolina Catholics*, 141; 1976 visit by author. In Powers, *Black Charlestonians*, there is no mention of relations with Irish Catholic educational efforts for blacks or Afro-American Catholics.
39. Gleeson, *Irish in the South*, 87; *State*, October 27, 2002.
40. Krebsbach, "Black Catholics."
41. Miller, "Roman Catholicism," 91, 96.
42. Mitchell, *Hibernian Society*, 54–57; *Irish-American*, December 30, 1849; Strum, "South Carolina."
43. Madden, *South Carolina Catholics*, 55; O'Connell, *Catholicity in South Carolina*.

44. Mitchell, *Hibernian Society*, 27, 57, 70; Silver, "Old South Urbanization."
45. Gleeson, *Irish in South*, 109, 118–19; Schultz, *Nationalism and Sectionalism*, 78–83; O'Connell, *Catholicity in South Carolina*, 247.
46. O'Connell, *Catholicity in South Carolina*, 340–50. Richard Madden says the building was occupied by Confederate deserters (*South Carolina Catholics*, 93).
47. O'Connell, *Catholicity in South Carolina*, 209. Douglass, *Narrative*; Maguire, *Irish in America*, 634–36.
48. Ignatiev, *Irish Became White*.
49. Maguire, *Irish in America*, 634–36; Bishop Lynch had several slaves, while Dr. O'Connell had one, who remained with him after emancipation. It would be a reasonable assumption that several priests owned slaves. O'Connell, *Catholicity in South Carolina*, 333; Gleeson, *Irish in the South*, 122–28.
50. Strum, "Famine," 132, 140.

Chapter 4

1. Gleeson, *Irish in the South*, 138; Madden, *South Carolina Catholics*, 81–82; *Charleston News and Courier*, December 8, 1929. The Leonard referred to was Captain Lauglin Leonard, who was killed during the Revolution in an attack on Haye's Station in November 1781. Moss, *South Carolina Patriots*, 563–64.
2. Mitchell, *Hibernian Society*, 54, 67–68, 100; Gleeson, *Irish in the South*, 159; Wikipedia, s.v. "Walsh"; Walsh, "Irish in South Carolina."
3. Madden, *South Carolina Catholics*, 82; O'Connell, *Catholicity in South Carolina*, 268.
4. Gleeson, *Irish in the South*, 154–55, 230 n. 68; *Irish Times* article quoted in *Galway-American*, September 27, 1862; Joyce, "Charleston's Irish Labourers."
5. Madden, *South Carolina Catholics*, 91–92; Heisser, "Bishop Lynch's," 681–96; Heisser, "Bishop Lynch."
6. O'Connell, *Catholicity in South Carolina*, 225–28; Gleeson, *Irish in South*, 159–60, 170.
7. McGovern, *John Mitchel*, 179–180, 180; Hibernian Society, *Minutes of Meetings*, March 17, 1869, 173–74.
8. Simms, *Paddy McGann*, vol. III, xix–xxi; Cantrell, "Irish Culture," 7–15; Mitchell, *Hibernian Society*, 27, 35, 51, 61–62; *Encyclopedia of South Carolina*, 115–16.

9. Gleeson, *Irish in the South*, 161. See also Wise, *Lifeline of the Confederacy.*
10. O'Connell, *Catholicity in South Carolina*, 251–61; Madden, *South Carolina Catholics*, 87.
11. Ibid., 87.
12. O'Connell, *Catholicity in South Carolina*, 269–81; Madden, *South Carolina Catholics*, 93–96.
13. Ibid., 97–98.

CHAPTER 5

1. Mitchell, *Hibernian Society*, 74; Hope and Silverman, *Relief and Recovery*, 82; *Southern Celt*, USC, Caroliniana Library collection.
2. Maguire, *Irish in America*, appendix, 625–28; 252–55; Jones, *South Carolina*, 554. Hope and Silverman, *Relief and Recovery*, 271–94. A renewed effort took place in the mid-1870s. Zuczek, *State of Rebellion*, 137. In the first decade of the twentieth century, state law provided financing of Scandinavian emigration (hence, the towns of Norway, Sweden, Denmark and Finland) until this measure was ruled unconstitutional in 1906.
3. "Hibernicus [James Power?]," letter in an Irish-American newspaper reprinted in *Irish People* [Dublin], August 12, 1865; Mitchell, *Hibernian Society*, 74–75; Power obituary, *Charleston News and Courier*, May 10, 1879.
4. Mitchell, *Hibernian Society*, 79–82; O'Connell, *Catholicity in South Carolina*, 170–74; O'Connor, *M.P. O'Connor*; Williams, *Shamrocks*, 128–31.
5. Gleeson, *Irish in the South*, 139, 181–86.
6. Madden, *Catholics in South Carolina.*
7. Burts, *Richard Irvine Manning*, 1–4.
8. Duffy, "Charleston Politics"; Boggs, "John Patrick Grace"; Fraser, *Charleston! Charleston!*, 428–36; Williams, *Shamrocks*, 136–46.
9. Byrnes, *All in One Lifetime.* Byrnes does not state that his parents were Irish immigrants but does examine his changing from the Catholic Church to the Episcopal denomination (see p. 16); Richard Riley interview. John J. Duffy's explanation of how Kennedy carried South Carolina was: "Fritz wanted him," referring to Senator Ernest F. Hollings.
10. AOH South Carolina State Board website; *State*, March 7, 2004, 2010; Doherty and Lawracy interviews.
11. In addition, the Charleston Historical Society sponsors an annual Irish in Charleston and South Carolina lecture during St. Patrick's week. On the

Charleston Irish Trail: Led by Stephen White, the group included David Heisser, David Fleeson, Nic Butler, Denis Bergin and Don Williams; Charleston Historical Society lecture; White interview.

12. AOH South Carolina State Board website; *State,* June 29, September 7, 2008; *Catholic Miscellany*, September 18, 2008.
13. "The Festival of Ballycahill," *Irish Arts Celebration*, March 12–17, 2010 program.
14. Berman, "From Potatoes to Politics."

Bibliography

South Carolina Irish

Reference Works and General Histories

Akenson, Donald. *The Irish Diaspora: A Primer*. Toronto: P.D. Meany, 1993.

Bielenberg, Andy, ed. *The Irish Diaspora.* New York: Longman, 2000.

Blessing, Patrick J. *The Irish in America: A Guide to the Literature and Manuscript Collections.* Washington, D.C.: Catholic U.P., 1992.

Boatner, Mark. *Encyclopedia of the American Revolution*. New York: David McKay, 1976.

Doyle, David, Kerby Miller, Arnold Schrier and Bruce Boling, eds. *Ireland, Irishmen and Revolutionary America, 1760–1820*. Dublin: Mercier Press, 1981.

———. *Irish Immigrants in the Land of Canaan: Letters and Memoirs from Colonial and Revolutionary America, 1765–1815*. Oxford, UK: Oxford University Press, 2003.

Easterby, J.H. *Guide to the Study and Reading of South Carolina History*. Supplement by Noel Polk. Spartanburg, SC: Reprint Company, 1975.

Edgar, Walter. *South Carolina; A History*. Columbia: University of South Carolina Press, 1998.

Edgar, Walter B., and N. Louise Bailey. *Biographical Directory of the South Carolina House of Representatives, vol. 2, the Commons House of Assembly, 1692–1775*. Columbia: University of South Carolina Press, n.d.

Editors of *Who's Who in America* with Jerry Kail. *Who Was Who During the American Revolution*. Indianapolis, IN: Bobbs Merrill, 1976.

Encyclopedia of South Carolina. New York: Somerset, 1993.

Glazier, Michael, ed. *Encylopedia of the Irish in America*. Notre Dame, IN: University of Notre Dame Press, 1999.

Hewatt, Alexander. *A Historical Account of the Rise and Progress of the Colonies of South Carolina and Georgia*. Spartanburg, SC: Reprint Company, 1962.

Jones, Lewis P. *Books and Articles on South Carolina History: A List for Laymen*. Columbia: University of South Carolina Press, 1970.

MacLysaght, Edward. *The Surnames of Ireland*. New York: Barnes and Noble, 1969.

McCrady, Edward. *The History of South Carolina in the Revolution, 1775–1780; 1780–2783*. New York: Macmillan, 1901, 1902.

———. *The History of South Carolina under the Proprietary Government, 1670–1719*. New York: Macmillan, 1897.

Meagher, Timothy. *The Columbia Guide to Irish American History*. New York: Columbia University Press, 2005.

Miller, Kerby. *Emigrants and Exiles: Ireland and the Irish Exodus to North America*. New York: Oxford University Press, 1985.

Miller, Kerby, Arnold Schrier, Bruce Boling and David Doyle, eds. *Irish Immigrants in the Land of Canaan: Letters and Memoirs from Colonial and Revolutionary America, 1675–1815*. New York: Oxford University Press, 2003.

Moore, John Hammond. *Research Materials in South Carolina; A Guide*. Columbia: University of South Carolina Press, 1967.

Neuffer, Claude. *Names in South Carolina*. Spartanburg, SC: Reprint Company, 1983.

Rivers, William J. *A Sketch of the History of South Carolina to the Close of the Proprietary Government*. Charleston, SC: McCarter, 1856.

Snowden, Yates, and H.G. Cutler. *History of South Carolina*. Chicago: Lewis Pub. Co, 1920.

Wallace, D.D. *History of South Carolina*. 4 vols. N.p., 1934.

———. *South Carolina; A Short History, 1520–1948*. Chapel Hill: University of North Carolina Press, 1951.

Primary Sources

Carolina described more fully than heretofore, being an impartial collection from the several relations of that place, since its first planting by the English and before under the denomination of Florida, from divers letters from the Irish settled there, and relations of those who have been there several years, whereunto is added the charter, with the fundamental constitution of that province, and etc.
—Dublin, 1684

Butler Family Papers, 1801–1991. USC Caroliniana Library Archives.
Henry C. Conner Papers, 1803–1882. College of Charleston Archives.
Dickson Family Papers, 1762–1932. College of Charleston Archives.
Glass Family Papers, 1758–1938. College of Charleston Archives.
Lynch Family Papers. USC Caroliniana Library.
Davison McDowell Papers, 1759–1958. College of Charleston Archives.
Molony, Bryan and Ryan Family Papers, 1838–1874. College of Charleston Archives.
Reynolds Family Papers, 1837–1958. USC Caroliniana Library.
Salley, A.S., ed. *Warrants for Lands in South Carolina, 1672-- 1711*. Columbia: University of South Carolina Press, 1972. [Reprint of 1910–15 original.]

Articles

Ahlstrom, J.D. "Captain and Chef de Brigade: William Tate, South Carolina Adventurer." *South Carolina Historical Magazine* (October 1987): 183–91.
———. "William Tate, South Carolina Adventurer." *South Carolina Historical Magazine* 88 (October 1987): 183–91.
Ames, Joseph S. "The Cantey Family." *South Carolina Historical Magazine* 11 (1910): 203–58.
Berman, Pat. "From Potatoes to Politics, S.C. Irish Roots Run Deep." *The State*, March 17, 1995.
Burke, Aedanus. "Address to the Freemen of South Carolina." Philadelphia, 1783.
Calhoon, Robert M. "Aedanus Burke and Thomas Burke: Revolutionary Conservatism in the Carolinas." In *The Meaning of South Carolina History: Essays in Honor of George C. Rogers Jr.* Edited by D. Chestnutt and C. Wilson. Columbia: University of South Carolina Press, 1991.
Carroll, Kenneth L. "The Irish Quaker Community at Camden." *South Carolina Historical Magazine* 77, no. 2 (1976): 69–83.

Chestnutt, David R., and Liza M. Floyd. "Sergeant Jasper: Hero of the Revolution." 1976.

Clark, Dennis. "The South's Irish Catholics: A Case of Cultural Confinement." In *Catholics in the Old South*. Edited by R. Miller and J. Wakelyn. Macon, GA, 1983.

Cobb, Irving. *The Lost Tribes of Irish in the South*. Washington, D.C.: Irish National Bureau, 1919.

Coghlan, Francis. "Pierce Butler, 1744–1822, First Senator from South Carolina." *South Carolina Historical Magazine* 78, no. 2 (April 1977): 104–19.

Cosgrave, John I. "The Hibernian Society of Charleston, South Carolina." *American Irish Historical Society Journal* 25 (1926).

Crary, Catherine. "Humble Immigrant and the American Dream." *Journal of American History* 46 (1959): 59–61.

Crowson, E. Thomas. "Building the Landsford Canal." *South Carolina History Illustrated* (May 1970): 19, 61.

Doherty, John. *Saint Andrews Chapel.* Booklet. Barnwell, SC, 1978.

Doyle, David. "The Scotch- Irish." In *Encylopedia of the Irish in America*. Edited by M. Glazier. Notre Dame, IN: University of Notre Dame Press, n.d.

Eid, Leroy. "The Colonial Scotch-Irish: A View Accepted Too Readily." *Eire/ Ireland* (Winter 1986): 81–1105.

———. "Irish, Scotch and Scotch-Irish, A Reconsideration." *American Presbyterians; Journal of Presbyterian History* 84, no. 4 (Winter 1986): 211–26.

Franklin, Elizabeth Downes. "History of American Women" blog. www.womenhistoryblog.com.

Garland, J.L. "The Irish Dragoons in the American Civil War." *Irish Sword: Journal of the Military History Society of Ireland* 1, no. 1 (1949–50): 37–39.

———. "Irish Soldiers of the Confederacy." *Irish Sword: Journal of the Military History Society of Ireland*, no. 3 (1951–52): 174–80.

Heisser, David. "Bishop Lynch's Civil War Pamphlet on Slavery: A Contribution to the Confederate Cause." *Catholic Historical Review* 84, no. 4 (1998): 681–96.

———. "Bishop Lynch's People: Slaveholding by a South Carolina Prelate." *South Carolina Historical Magazine* 102, no. 3 (July 2001): 238–62.

———. "Bishop Patrick Lynch and the Confederacy." In *Irish Soldiers, American Wars: Irish Participation in the Mexican and American Civil Wars*. Edited by A. Mitchell and D. Doyle. Dublin: Irish Academic Press, 2011.

Joyce, Dee Dee. "Charleston's Irish Labourers and Their Move into the Confederacy." *Irish Studies Review* 18, no. 2 (May 2010): 185–97.

Kenny, Michael. "The Irish in 'The South.'" *Studies* [Dublin] 22 (1933): 89–100.

Kilber, James. "Simms's Irish: An Address at Hibernian Society Hall, Charleston, South Carolina, 14 January 1999." *Simms Review* 9, no. 2 (1999): 1–7.

"Kingston-Conway/Robert Conway Marker." Historical Marker Database. www.hmdb.org/marker.asp?marker=11291

Lees, William B. "The Historical Development of Limerick Plantation." *South Carolina Historical Magazine* 82, no. 2 (January 1981): 44–47.

McCrady, Edward. Obituary. *SCHGM* 5 (1904): 62.

McWhiney, Grady. "The Irish Heritage of the American South." In *Selected Proceedings of Scotch-Irish Heritage Festival, II at Winthrop College*. Edited by Jack Weaver. Baton Rouge, LA, 1984.

Melvin, Patrick. "Captain Florence O'Sullivan and the Origins of Carolina." *South Carolina Historical Magazine*, 76 (1975): 235–49.

———. "John Barnwell and Colonial South Carolina." *Irish Sword: The Journal of the Military History Society of Ireland* 11, no. 42: 5–20; no. 43: 129–41.

Miller, Kerby. "'Scotch-Irish,' 'Black Irish' and 'Real Irish': Emigrants and Identities in the Old South." In *The Irish Diaspora*. Edited by Andy Bielenberg. Harlow, England, 2000.

Miller, Randal. "The Enemy Within: Some Effects of Foreign Immigrants on Antebellum Southern Cities." *Southern Studies* 24 (Spring 1985): 32–33.

———. "Roman Catholicism in South Carolina." In *Religion in South Carolina*. Edited by Charles Lippy. Columbia: University of South Carolina Press, 1993.

———. "Andrew Jackson." In *Encyclopedia of the Irish in America*. Edited by Michael Glazier. Notre Dame, IN: University of Notre Dame Press, 1999.

———. "The Irish in South Carolina." In *Encyclopedia of the Irish in America*. Edited by Michael Glazier. Notre Dame, IN: University of Notre Dame Press, 1999.

Mitchell, Arthur. "Irishmen and the American Revolution." *Capuchin Annual* (1976).

———. "James F. Byrnes." In *Encyclopedia of the Irish in America*. Edited by Michael Glazier. Notre Dame, IN: University of Notre Dame Press, 1999.

Morris, Richard B. "White Bondage in Ante- bellum South Carolina." *SCHGM* 49 (1948): 194–95.

O'Brien, Michael J. "The Irish in Charleston, South Carolina." *American Irish Historical Society* 25 (1926): 134–46.

———. "Irish in South Carolina." *American Irish Historical Society* 25 (1926).

———. "Limerick Plantation, Berkeley County, South Carolina." *American Irish Historical Society* 25 (1926).

———. "Marriage Notices Published in the South Carolina Gazette." *American Irish Historical Society* 25 (1926).

O'Connor, Edward T. "Michael Tuomey, 1805–1857." *American Irish Historical Journal* 30 (1932): 71–74.

Reville, Janie. *560 Irish Immigrants Who Came to South Carolina in 1768.* Pamphlet. Caroliniana Library, Columbia, SC, 1937.

Roper, Louis. "The Unraveling of an Anglo-American Utopia in South Carolina." *The Historian* 58, no. 2 (Winter 1996): 277–88.

Rousey, Dennis. "Aliens in the WASP Nest: Ethnocultural Diversity in the Antebellum South." *Journal of American History* 79 (June 1992): 154–57.

Salley, A.S. "The Calhoun Family of South Carolina." *South Carolina Historical Magazine* 11 (1910): 158–63, 248–50; 7 (1906): 81–98, 153–69; 39 (1938): 50.

Seale, William, ed. "James Hoban: Builder of the White House." *White House History* 22 (Spring 2008): 4–17.

Shy, John. "American Society and Its War of Independence." In *Reconsiderations of the Revolutionary War.* Edited by Don Higginbotham. Westport, CT: Greenwood Press, 1978.

Silk, John J. "The Irish Abroad in the Age of the Counter-Reformation, 1549–1691." In *A New History of Ireland; III: Early Modern Ireland.* Edited by T.W. Moody, F.X. Martin and F.J. Byrne. Oxford: Clarendon Press, 1976.

Silver, Christopher. "A New Look at Old South Urbanization: The Irish Worker in Charleston, South Carolina, 1840–1860." In *South Atlantic Urban Studies.* Vol. 3. Edited by Samuel Hines and George Hopkins. Columbia: University of South Carolina Press, 1979.

Smith, Henry. "The Baronies of South Carolina." *SCHGM* 18 (1917): 3–36.

Snoddy, Oliver. "The Volunteers of Ireland." *The Irish Sword* (Winter 1965): 137–39.

Strum, Harvey. "South Carolina and Irish Famine Relief, 1846–47." *South Carolina Historical Magazine* 103, no. 2 (April 2002): 130–52.

Thomas, Samuel. *The Dye Is Cast: The Scots-Irish and the Revolution in the Carolina Back Country.* Columbia, SC: Palmetto Conservation Foundation, 1997.

Walsh, Patrick. "The Irish in South Carolina, Georgia, Alabama, Louisiana and Tennessee." *American Irish Historical Society Journal* 3 (1900).

Walsh, Richard. "Edmund Egan: Charleston's Rebel Brewer." *SCHGM* 56 (1955): 200–04.

Books by Contemporaries

Collins, James P. *Autobiography of a Revolutionary Soldier*. New York: Arno Press, 1972.

Drayton, John. *Memoirs of the American Revolution*. 2 vols. Charleston, SC, 1821.

Garden, Alexander. *Anecdotes of the Revolutionary War in America with Sketches of the Most Distinguished, in the Southern States, for Civil and Military Services*. Charleston, SC, 1882.

Hewett, Alexander. *A Historical Account of the Rise and Progress of the Colonies of South Carolina and Georgia*. 2 vols. London, 1779.

O'Connell, J.J. *Catholicity in the Carolinas and Georgia*. New York: D. and J. Sadlier, 1879. Reprint, Spartanburg, SC: Reprint Company, 1972.

Ramsay, David. *The History of the American Revolution*. 2 vols. Philadelphia, 1793.

———. *Ramsay's History of South Carolina; from the First Settlement in 1670 to the Year 1808*. Charleston, SC, 1809. Reprint, Spartanburg, SC, 1959.

Simms, William Gilmore. *The Writings of William Gilmore Simms*. Vol. 2. Columbia: University of South Carolina Press, 1972.

Woodmason, Charles. *The Carolina Backcountry on the Eve of the Revolution; The Journal and Other Writings of Charles Woodmason, Anglican Itinerant*. Edited by Richard J. Hooker. Chapel Hill: University of North Carolina Press, 1953.

Books, Later Works

Armstrong, James. *Portrayal of an Eventful Past*. Pamphlet. Charleston, 1917. [History of St. Patrick's Benevolent Society.]

Ball, Edward. *Slaves in the Family*. New York : Farrar, Straus and Giroux, 1998.

Bernheim, G.D. *History of the German Settlers and of the Lutheran Church in North and South Carolina, from the Earliest Period of the Colonization of the Dutch, German and Swiss Settlers to the Close of the First Half of the Present Century*. Baltimore, MD: Genealogical Publishing, 1996.

Bridenbaugh, Carl. *Cities in Revolt: Urban Life in America, 1743–1776*. New York: Knopf, 1965.

Brown, Richard M. *The South Carolina Regulators*. Cambridge, MA: Belknap Press, 1963.

Burts, Robert M. *Richard Irvine Manning and the Progressive Movement in South Carolina*. Columbia: University of South Carolina Press, 1974.

Cantrell, James P. *How Celtic Culture Invented Southern Literature*. Gretna, LA: Pelican Publishing, 2006.

Carroll, Bartholomew R. *Historical Collections of South Carolina.* 2 vols. New York, 1836.

Cash, Wilbur J. *The Mind of the South.* New York: Knopf, 1941. [Later edition with introduction by Denis Brogan, 1954.]

Chalkley, Lyman. *Chronicles of the Scotch-Irish Settlement in Virginia, Extracted from the Original Court Records of Augusta County, 1745–1800.* Baltimore, MD: Genealogical Publishing, 1965.

Cohen, Hennig, ed. *South Carolina Gazette, 1732–1775.* Columbia: University of South Carolina Press, 1953.

Coit, Margaret L. *John C. Calhoun: American Portrait.* Boston: Houghton Mifflin, 1950.

Crane, Verner. *The Southern Frontier: 1670–1733.* Durham, NC: Duke University Press, 1929.

Dabney, William H., and Marion Dargan. *William Henry Drayton and the American Revolution.* Albuquerque: University of New Mexico Press, 1962.

Doyle, David N. *Ireland, Irishmen and Revolutionary America, 1760–1820.* Cork, Ireland: Mercier Press, 1981.

Gibbes, R.W., ed. *Documentary History of the American Revolution.* Vol. 3, *1781–82.* Spartanburg, SC: Reprint Company, 1972.

Gleeson, David T. *The Irish in the South, 1815–1877.* Chapel Hill: University of North Carolina Press, 2001.

Griffin, Martin. *Catholics and the American Revolution.* Ridley Park, PA, 1907.

Griffin, Patrick. *The People of No Name: Ireland's Ulster Scots, America's Scots Irish and the Creation of a British Atlantic World, 1689–1764.* Princeton, NJ: Princeton University Press, 2001.

Guilday, Peter K. *The Life and Times of John England.* 2 vols. New York, 1927.

Howe, George. *History of the Presbyterian Church in South Carolina.* Vol. 1. Columbia, SC, 1870.

———. *The Scotch-Irish and the First Settlements of the Tyger River and Other Neighboring Precincts in South Carolina.* Booklet. Columbia, SC, 1861.

Ignatiev, Noel. *How the Irish Became White.* New York: Routledge, 1995.

Johnson, Joseph. *Traditions and Reminiscences Chiefly of the American Revolution in the South.* Charleston, SC, 1851. Reprint, Spartanburg, SC: Reprint Company, 1972.

Jones, Patricia K. *Across the Ocean of Promise; the Irish of Charleston, South Carolina.* Oakwood, GA, 2006.

Joyce, Dee Dee. "White, Worker, Irish and Confederate: Irish Workers Constructed Identity in Late Antebellum Charleston, South Carolina." PhD diss., State University of New York at Binghamton, New York, 2002.

Killion, Ronald G., and Bobby G. Moss, eds. *The Journal of Michael Gaffney: From Ireland to the Backwoods of South Carolina*. Greenville, SC: A Press, 1981.

Lambert, Robert S. *South Carolina Loyalists in the American Revolution*. Columbia: University of South Carolina Press, 1987.

Landrum, John B. *Colonial and Revolutionary History of Upper South Carolina*. Spartanburg, SC: Reprint Company, 1977.

Lawson, John. *A New Voyage to Carolina*. Ann Arbor, MI: University Microfilms, 1966.

Lockhart, Audrey. *Some Aspects of Emigration from Ireland to North American Colonies Between 1660 and 1775*. New York: Arno Press, 1976.

Logan, John H. *History of the Upper Country of South Carolina*. Charleston, SC, 1859.

Madden, Richard C. *Catholics in South Carolina*. New York: Lanham, 1985.

Maguire, John Francis. *The Irish in America*. London: Longmans Green, 1868. [See Bishop Lynch's letter to Maguire in Appendix.]

Meleney, John C. *The Public Life of Aedanus Burke: Revolutionary Republican in Post-Revolutionary South Carolina*. Columbia: University of South Carolina Press, 1989.

Meriwether, Robert L. *The Expansion of South Carolina, 1729–1765*. Kingsport, TN: Southern Publishers, 1940.

Metzger, Charles H. *Catholics and the American Revolution: A Study in Religious Climate*. Chicago: Loyola University Press, 1962.

Miller, John C. *Origins of the American Revolution*. Boston: Little Brown, 1943.

Miller, Kerby. *Emigrants and Exiles: Ireland and the Irish Exodus to North America*. New York, 1985.

Mitchell, Arthur, ed. *The History of the Hibernian Society of Charleston, S.C., 1799–1981*. Charleston, SC: Hibernian Society, 1982.

———. *Ireland and Irishmen in the American War of Independence: Some Historical Documents*. Dublin: Academy Press, 1976. [Reproductions of original documents.]

Moore, J.H. *Columbia and Richland County: A South Carolina Community, 1740–1990*. Columbia: University of South Carolina Press, 1993.

Moore, Maurice A. *Life of General Edward Lacey*. Greenville, SC: A. Press, 1981.

Moore, Peter N. *This World of Toil and Strife: Land, Labor and the Making of an American Community*. Columbia: University of South Carolina Press, 2007.

Moss, Bobby G., ed. *Roster of South Carolina Patriots in the American Revolution*. Baltimore, MD: Genealogical Publishing, 1983.

Motes, Margaret Peckham. *Irish Found in South Carolina 1850 Census*. N.p.: Clearfield Company, 2003.

Nadelhart, Jerome J. *The Disorders of War: The Revolution in South Carolina*. Orono: University of Maine Press, 1981.

O'Brien, Michael J. *A Hidden Phase of American History: Ireland's Part in America's Struggle for Liberty*. Baltimore, MD, 1973.

O'Neall, John Belton. *Annals of Newberry*. Charleston, SC, 1859.

———. *Biographical Sketches of the Bench and Bar of South Carolina*. Spartanburg, SC: Reprint Company, 1975.

Osborne, Anne Riggs. *The South Carolina Story*. Orangeburg, SC: Sandlapper, 1988.

O Snodaigh, Padraig. *Hidden Ulster: Protestants and the Irish Language*. Belfast: Lagan Press, 1995. [Name Snoddy in Gaelic.]

Palmer, Gregory. *Biographical Sketches of Loyalists of the American Revolution*. London, 1984.

Pope, Thomas H. *The History of Newberry County, South Carolina, 1749–1860*. Columbia: University of South Carolina Press, 1973.

Ramsey, Robert. *Carolina Cradle: Settlement of the Northwest Carolina Frontier, 1747–1762*. Chapel Hill: University of North Carolina Press, 1964.

Ray, Mary Augustina. *American Opinion of Roman Catholicism in the Eighteenth Century*. New York: Columbia University Press, 1936. Reprint, New York: Octagon Books, 1974.

Rosen, Robert N. *A Short History of Charleston*. San Francisco, CA: Lexikos, 1982.

Rosen, Robert N., and Isabella Leland. *Charleston: Crossroads of History*. Sun Valley, CA: American Historical Press, n.d.

Rossiter, Clinton. *The First American Revolution: The American Colonies on the Eve of Independence*. New York: Harcourt, 1953.

Shy, John. *A People Numerous and Armed: Reflections on the Military Struggle for American Independence*. London: Oxford University Press, 1976.

Simms, William Gilmore. *Life of General Francis Marion*. New York, 1844.

———. *The Revolutionary War in South Carolina: An Anthology*. Compiled by Stephen Meets. 2 vols. Columbia: Southern Studies Program, University of South Carolina, 1975.

Sirmans, M. Eugene. *Colonial South Carolina: A Political History, 1663–1763*. Chapel Hill: University of North Carolina Press, 1966.

Smith, Warren B. *White Servitude in Colonial South Carolina*. Columbia: University of South Carolina Press, 1961.

Taylor, Rosser H. *Ante-Bellum South Carolina: A Social and Cultural History*. New York: DaCapo Press, 1970.

Thomas, Samuel. *The Dye is Cast: The Scots-Irish and Revolution in the Carolina Back Country*. Columbia, SC: Palmetto Conservation Foundation, 1997.

Tobin, William. *The Irish in South Carolina*. Booklet, Florence, SC, circa 1930s.

Typescript. A huge compilation of names based on the U.S. census of 1850, a copy of which is in the National Library of Ireland (ref. 7B 336).

Walsh, Richard. *Charleston's Sons of Liberty; A Study of the Artisans, 1763–1789*. Columbia: University of South Carolina Press, 1959.

Waring, Joseph I. *The First Voyage and Settlement at Charles Town, 1670–1680*. Tercentennial booklet, no. 4. Columbia: University of South Carolina Press, 1970.

Watterson, John S. *Thomas Burke: Restless Revolutionary*. Washington, D.C., 1980.

Weaver, Jack, ed. *Selected Proceeding of the Scotch-Irish Festival at Winthrop College, 1980*. Winthrop College, SC, 1981.

———. *Selected Proceedings of the Scotch-Irish Festival at Winthrop College II, 1983*. Baton Rouge, LA: VAAPR, 1984.

Weigley, Russell. *The Partisan War: The South Carolina Campaign of 1780–1782*. Columbia: University of South Carolina Press, 1970.

White, Katherine Keogh. *The King's Mountain Men*. Dayton, VA, 1924.

Williams, Donald M. *Shamrocks and Pluff Mud: A Glimpse of the Irish in the Southern City of Charleston, South Carolina*. Charleston, SC: self-published, 2005.

Wilson, David A. *United Irishmen, United States: Immigrant Radicals in the Early Republic*. Dublin: Four Courts Press, 1998.

Wood, Gordon S. *The Radicalism of the American Revolution*. New York: Knopf, 1993.

Wood, Peter. *Black Majority: Negroes in Colonial South Carolina: From 1607 to the Stono Rebellion.* New York: Norton, 1975.

Interviews and Communications

Bergin, Denis

Bingay, Mary Patricia McPhail

Condon, Irvin

Condon, Thomas

Darcy, Francis

David, Maria

Doherty, Joseph

Dougherty, Joseph

Doyle, David N.
Duffy, John J.
Duffy, Michael Patrick
Gleeson, David
Heisser, David
Joyce, Dee Dee
Lawracy, James
McDermott, Thomas
O Snodaigh, Padraig
Pulkinen, Carl
Riley, Joseph Patrick
Riley, Richard W.
Thomas, Andrew
Weaver, Jack
White, Stephen J.
Williams, Donald M.
Woods, Christopher John

Dissertations

Boggs, Doyle Willard, Jr. "John Patrick Grace and the Politics of Reform in South Carolina, 1900–1931." PhD diss., University of South Carolina, 1977.

Duffy, John J. "Charleston Politics in the Progressive Era." PhD diss., University of South Carolina, 1963.

Papers Presented at Conferences and Lectures

Bergin, Denis. "Charleston's Irish Architects." Irish in Atlantic World conference, College of Charleston, February 27–March 2, 2007.

Gleeson, David. "Irish Network in 19th century Charleston, S.C." American Conference on Irish Studies annual meeting, St. Paul, MN, 2003.

McMasters, Richard K. "Torrans and Poaug: Charleston's Merchants and Emigration from Ulster." Irish in Atlantic World conference, 2007.

Mitchell, Arthur. "The Irish in South Carolina." South Carolina Irish History Society, Charleston, SC, 2005.

Thompson, Michael D. "Irish and Black Labor Competition and the Changing Composition of Charleston's Antebellum Waterfront Community." Irish in Atlantic World conference, 2007.

IRISH IN NORTH CAROLINA

Articles

Dougherty Joseph. "Corner of Ireland in America." *Irish America*, July 21, 2010.

Green, E.R.R. "The Scotch-Irish and the Coming of the Revolution in North Carolina." *Irish Historical Studies* 7 (n.d.): 77–86.

McWhiney, Grady. "The Irish Heritage of the American South." *Proceedings of Scotch-Irish Festival* (1983).

Miller, Kerby. "'Scotch- Irish,' 'Real Irish' and 'Black Irish': Immigrants and Identities in the Old South." In *The Irish Diaspora*. Edited by A. Bielenberg. Longman, NY, 2000.

Powell, William S. "North Carolina." In *Encyclopedia of the Irish in America*. Edited by M. Glazier. Notre Dame, IN: University of Notre Dame Press, 1999.

Books

Blethen, Tyler, and Curtis Wood, eds. *Ulster and North America: Transatlantic Perspectives on the Scotch-Irish*. Tuscaloosa: University of Alabama Press, 1997.

Boatner, Mark. *Encyclopedia of the America Revolution*. New York: Donald McKay, 1976.

Connor, R.D.W. *Race Elements in the White Population of North Carolina*. Raleigh, NC, 1920.

Ekirch, A. Roger. *"Poor Carolina": Politics and Society in Colonial North Carolina, 1729–1776*. Chapel Hill: University of North Carolina Press, 1981.

Fenn, Elizabeth. *Natives and Newcomers: The Way We Lived in North Carolina before 1770*. Chapel Hill: University of North Carolina Press, 1983.

Kane, J.N, and G.L. Alexander. *Nicknames and Sobriquets of U.S. Cities, States and Counties*. Metuchen, NJ: Scarecrow Press, 1979.

Lefler, Hugh T., and William S. Powell. *Colonial North Carolina: A History*. New York, 1973.

Leyburn, James G. *The Scotch-Irish: A Social History*. Chapel Hill, NC, 1962.

McDonnell, John, and James MacSparran. In *Irish Immigrants in the Land of Canaan; Letters and Memoirs from Colonial and Revolutionary America, 1675–1815*. Edited and composed by Kerby Miller, Arnold Schrier, Bruce Bolling and David Doyle. London: Oxford University Press, 2003.

Powell, William S., ed. *Dictionary of North Carolina Biography*. 6 vols. Chapel Hill, NC, 1979–1996.

———. *North Carolina Through Four Centuries*. Chapel Hill, NC, 1989.

Powers, William F. *Tar Heel Catholics: A History of Catholicism in North Carolina*. Lanham, MD: University Press of America, 2003.

Ramsey, Robert W. *Carolina Cradle: Settlement of the Northwest Carolina Frontier, 1747–1762*. Chapel Hill, NC, 1964.

Watterson, John Sayle *Thomas Burke: Restless Revolutionary*. Washington, D.C.: University Press of America, 1980.

Worsley, Stephen C. "Catholicism in Antebellum North Carolina." *North Carolina Historical Review* 60 (October 1983).

Thomas Burke

Calhoon, Robert M. "Aedanus Burke and Thomas Burke: Revolutionary Conservatism in the Carolinas." In *The Meaning of South Carolina History: Essays in Honor of George C. Rogers, Jr*. Edited by David Chestnutt and Clyde Wilson. Columbia: University of South Carolina Press, 1991.

Commanger, Henry Steele, and Richard B. Morris, eds. *The Spirit of Seventy-Six*. Indianapolis, IN: Bobbs-Merrill, 1958.

Dictionary of American Biography. New York: Scribner, 1990.

Miller, Kerby. *Emigrants and Exiles; Ireland and the Irish Exodus to North America*. New York: Oxford University Press, 1985.

Ray, Mary Augustina. *American Opinion of Roman Catholicism in the Eighteenth Century*. New York: Octagon Books, 1974. [Ray says that although there is no documentary evidence on the matter, there is a well-established tradition that Burke was a Catholic.]

Watterson, John S. *Thomas Burke: Restless Revolutionary*. Washington, D.C.: University Press of America, 1980.

About the Author

Arthur Mitchell, a native of Boston, received his undergraduate degree from Boston University and his PhD from the University of Dublin, where he honed his love of Irish history. Since 1976, he has been a history professor at the Salkehatchie Campus of the University of South Carolina at Allendale and Walterboro. Among his published works are *Labour in Irish Politics*, *Revolutionary Government in Ireland* and, along with coeditor Padraig O Snodaigh, two volumes of *Irish Politics Documents, 1869–1949*, with a departure into modern German history in a study of Hitler's links to Berchtesgaden and the Obersalzberg. His works relating to the Irish in America include a collection of documents about Irish involvement in the American Revolution, the Irish connections of John F. Kennedy, a history of the Hibernian Society of Charleston and, forthcoming, along with coeditor David Doyle, a collection of articles about Irish involvement in American wars. Moving further afield, he currently is writing a history of the Korean War. He was the 2010 recipient of the Irish Carolinian award by three Irish societies in Charleston.